Pinch Me

I Must Be Dreaming

Pinch Me

I Must Be Dreaming

ROBERT MANG

508 West 26th Street KEARNEY, NE 68848
402-819-3224
info@medialiteraryexcellence.com

CONTENTS

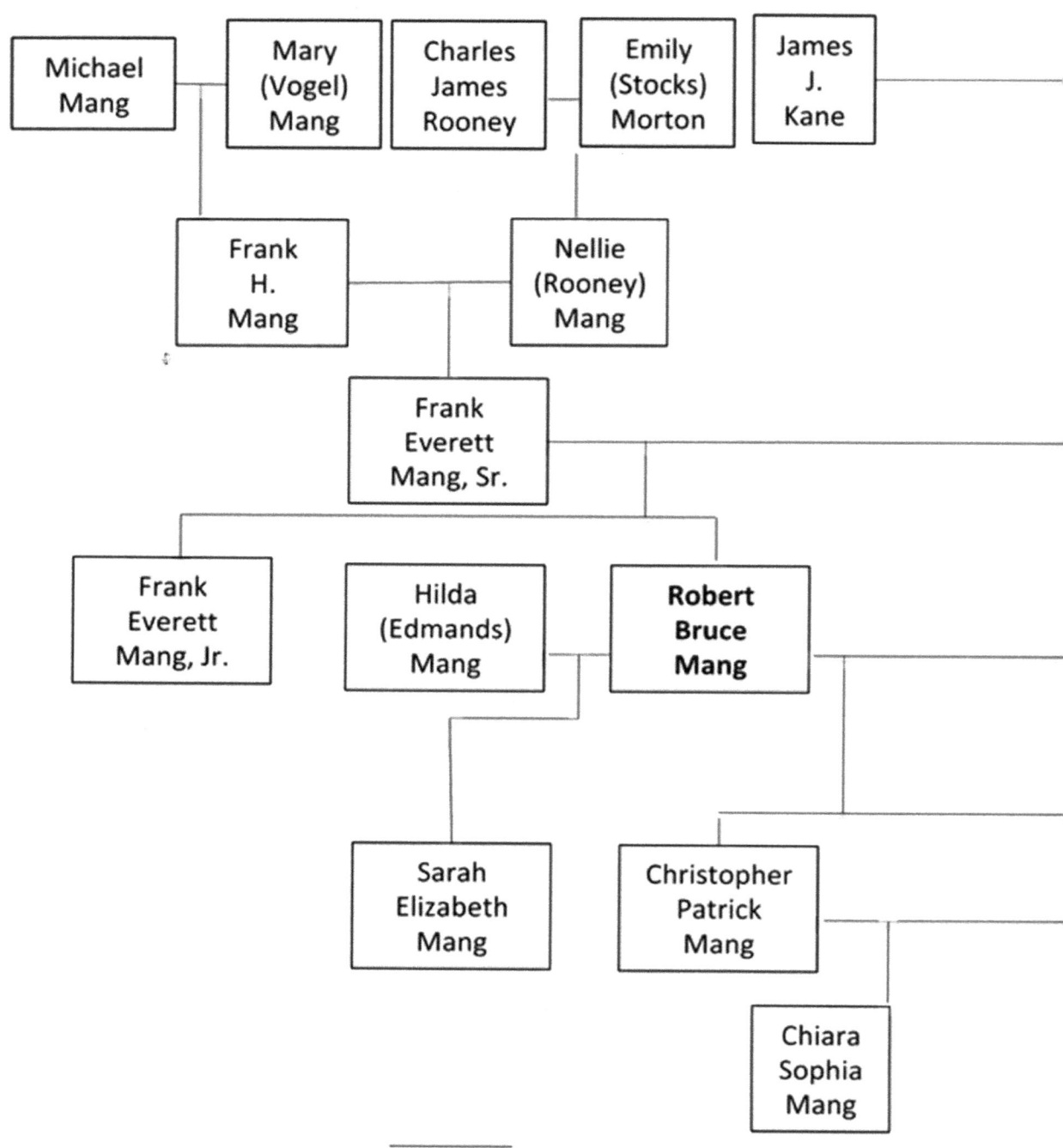

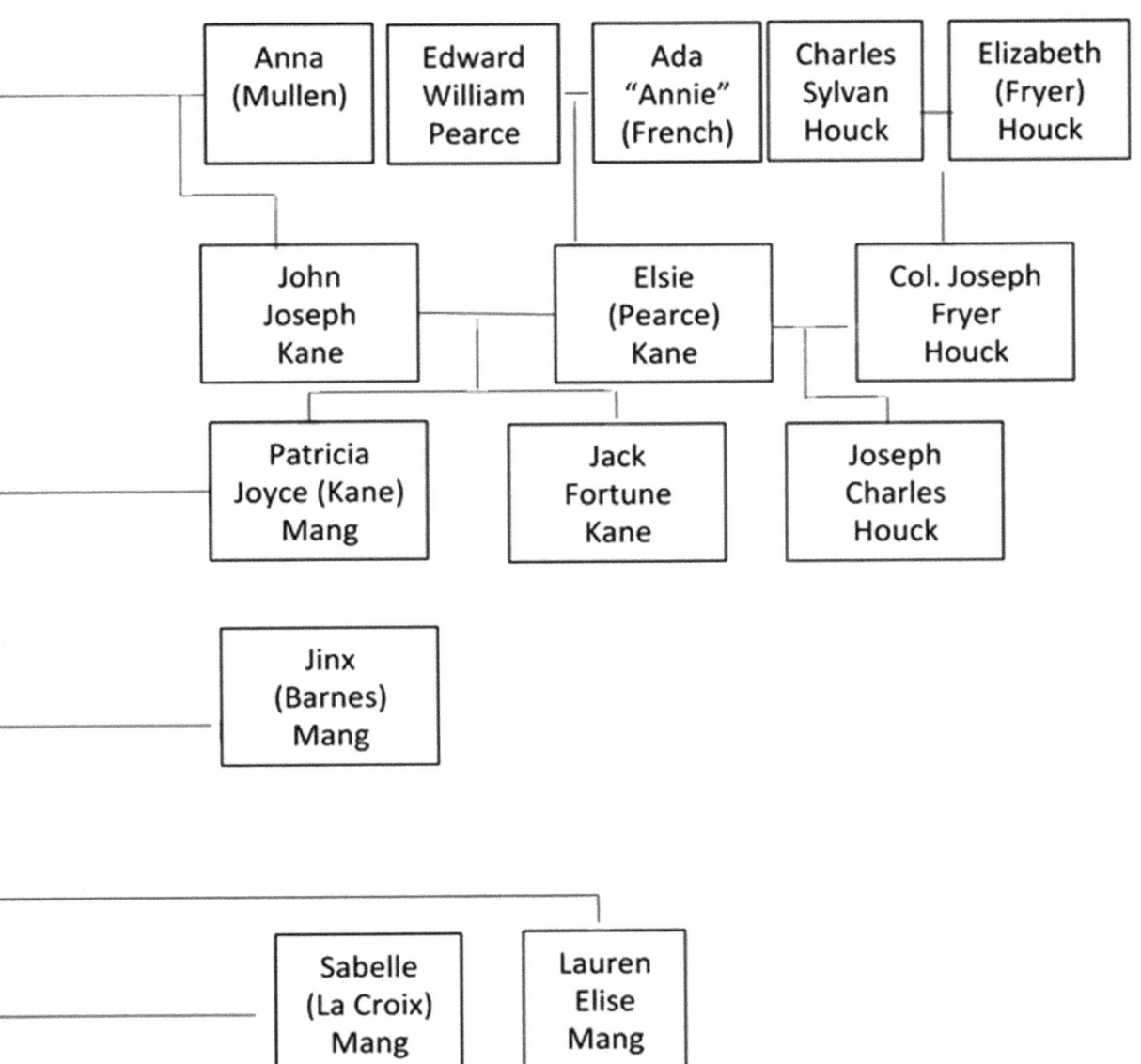

For
Chiara Sophia Mang.
May all her dreams come true.

FOREWORD

I was fortunate to read an early draft of Bob's memoir, as he was asking a few friends to give him some thoughts. I became so enthusiastic about it that I overreached my role as friend commenter, resulting in some wonderful conversations with Bob about his life and experiences.

When I first started reading, I thought that this was primarily a book about Bob the business man. His business career was not only successful but also spanned a period of enormous change in retailing, requiring the need for constant adaption and leadership. Through his many job changes, with increasing responsibility, you can track the movement in retailing from large urban department stores to the growth of store anchored suburban malls to specialty stores and to category killer, big box retailers like Galyan's (now Dicks Sporting Goods). Luckily, he retired and just missed the rise of the internet shopping boom! You can also see how disruptive this process was as Bob successfully demonstrated leadership both in company mergers and bankruptcies. And remember, this was going on during one of the most tumultuous times in our country's history (assassinations, civil rights movement, women's rights movement, Cold War then Vietnam War, all the protest movements, technological revolutions, etc.).

These pages also read like a "who's who" of retailing giants covering most, if not all, of the major players in US retailing. It is a story of them recognizing and growing Bob's talent and Bob, in turn, identifying and developing talent that would support his success. The challenges that they faced, the hard work required, the fun they had and the loyalty that was engendered in this process reflects well on Bob's character and ability to find, motivate and lead talented people. Treating people well and fairly, building a team, taking calculated risks, being willing to fail and learn, are all hallmarks of Bob's business career…and life.

But this is not just a business book. It is importantly also about family and friends. Bob's personal life was filled with the agony and the ecstasy of life (good parents, a challenging first marriage, a joyous second marriage, children (and grandchild), great friendships, wonderful trips, medical trauma and grief, creating a new life in retirement, etc.). I was struck by how many location changes Bob made over his career and the turmoil this can create for family, especially children. Chris, Lauren and Elizabeth, with the nurturing of their parents, seem to have survived this experience with only the typical bumps and bruises of the passage to adulthood. The loss of beloved parents, challenges besetting Jinx and the tragic death of Hilda were sad and traumatic experiences in Bob's life. However, Bob relates so many stories about fun vacations and exciting events over the years that his fundamental "joie de vivre" is ever present. His love of Florida State University for "changing his life" is palpable and reflected in the many actions he has taken to support the school over the years. The values of hard work, education, honesty, loyalty, friendship and love are all reflected here and encouraged in future generations.

I hope Bob's family and friends enjoy reading about Bob's life as much as I did.

Bob Patterson

Friend of Bob

P.S. I hope Bob continues to work on his golf game!

ACKNOWLEDGMENTS

Special thanks to my darling Ann, who kept pushing me to write this story; my great friend Larry Stack, who convinced me that I could write; Bob Patterson, who helped me edit my manuscript; and my amazing son, Chris, and his beautiful wife, Sabelle, who worked hand in hand with me to complete this project, the story of my life.

PROLOGUE

Without a doubt, my mother was the major influence in my life. Most, if not all, of my values are the result of her unconditional love and unwavering willingness to inspire me with the wisdom of her values—the foundation of my moral being. Primary was her belief in the golden rule: "Treat others as you would have others treat you." She set the standard for me in parenting, the single most important role in life. She taught me that the true test of character is how we face life's problems and focus on joy and fulfillment.

She taught me to reach for the stars I might just catch one. She was right. As you'll see, I caught more than my fair share of stars. So "pinch me! I must be dreaming" would be the best possible phrase to describe my amazing journey through life.

Patricia Joyce Mang
circa 1948

Patricia Joyce Mang
circa 2004

PAT AND FRANK

Patricia (Pat) Joyce Kane was a woman ahead of her time. She was born on February 29, 1924 (leap day of leap year), in New York City. At some point during her childhood, her mother, Nana, remarried (a dentist in the army), and the family moved to suburban Philadelphia. When she was thirteen, her brother, Joseph (Joe) Charles Houck, was born. She loved horseback riding and reveled in riding along the Schuylkill River in Philadelphia.

During WWII, she worked in a factory as an efficiency manager and later had quite a career in department store retailing, first as a service manager in the big-ticket area of the John Wanamaker (JW) Wynnewood store. Later, she worked for Burdines in Florida, as well as Macy's.

Frank Everett Mang was born on November 29, 1921, also in New York City. My grandfather Frank H. Mang had abandoned his family when my father was six or seven. Sometime in the 1930s, he and his mother (Nellie) moved to Upper Darby, where I was eventually born. On September 7, 1943, he was inducted into the United States Army Air Force. On January 15, 1944, Frank and Pat were married in Sioux Falls, South Dakota.

By January 31, 1945, my father was on his way to England, assigned to the 550th Bomb Squadron of the 385th Bomb Group of the Eighth Air Force. He was further assigned to 2nd Lt. Kenneth G. Tipton as the radioman on a B-17 nicknamed *Sugar Jo*. On only their second mission on Friday, March 2, 1945, their plane was hit by flak over Oschatz, Germany, and the crew was forced to bail out. German soldiers, who had beaten my father badly, captured them, and he was heavily interrogated because of his German surname. As the Allies advanced the front against the Nazis, the prisoners of war were forced to move and contained in open fields by barbed wire. During a hundred-mile march, my father connected with his high school buddy Bob (Robert Bruce) Forstburg, after whom I am named.

On April 29, 1945, Gen. George Patton's tank command liberated my father and the other prisoners. He rode in on a tank to thunderous cheers. My father was back on American soil in July of 1945, and my mother was seven months pregnant. He was discharged on November 18, 1945, and awarded the Purple Heart, the American Service Medal, the European–African–Middle Eastern Service Medal, the Good Conduct Medal, and the WWII Victory Medal.

Frank & Patricia Mang Wedding
January 15, 1944

Robert Bruce Forstburg &
Patricia Mang

Frank Mang
8th Marmy Air Force

Patricia & Frank Mang

EARLY BOOMER

Nobody really knows where their life's journey will take them or what their destiny might be, but every day has been a new adventure, and mine began at 7:05 p.m., September 30, 1945. I was born at Delaware County Hospital, in Upper Darby, Pennsylvania, right next door to where my parents attended high school.

My parents lived in a small apartment in Drexel Hill for the first few years of my life. Honestly, I have little—if any—recollection of those years. On December 13, 1947, a new intruder entered my life, Frank (Frankie) Everett Mang Jr. At that point, my parents began to search for larger accommodations not just for us but also to include my mother's mother (Elsie/Nana) and my mother's younger brother (Joe). Joe would become a major influence in my life and was much more of a big brother than an uncle.

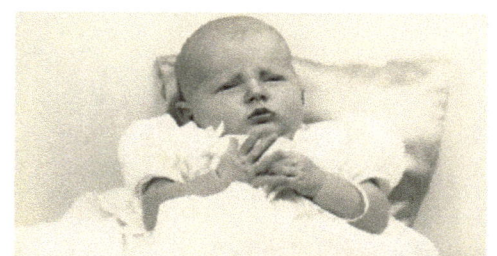

Robert Bruce Mang
Christening

Bob & Cousin Jackie

Bob pushing sled

Frank & Bob Mang

Pat & Bob Mang

Pat & Bob Mang

WILDE AVENUE

Sometime in the late '40s, we moved from Drexel Court Apartments to 211 Wilde Avenue, a row house duplex neighborhood not far away. Mom, Dad, Nana, Joe, Frankie, and I seemed very happy there. Joe took me to the circus when I was about five. I was awestruck. We actually watched them pitch the tent (a.k.a. the big top). I was amazed with the animals and the clowns and blown away by how many clowns they could stuff into that tiny little car.

I made my first friends there: Joanne Kelly (the girl next door), Denise Polthier, Howard McIlvane, Danny Seal (who got polio), Johnny Blair, and Shelley Bernstein, who slammed a door on my middle finger and broke it. I enjoyed lots of wonderful moments there—skipping down the sidewalk while singing at the top of my lungs, learning to ride my bike in the alley behind the house, sledding, climbing trees, and all the things carefree youngsters got to do. We had a small Philco TV and only got three channels. The transmissions were black and white and very snowy. My favorite show was *Howdy Doody*.

Television had captured the attention of the American public and greatly influenced my generation. In the '50s during the late-afternoon, early-evening hours, local shows were broadcast. (Westerns were very popular starring Gene Autry, "the Singing Cowboy," and the Cisco Kid.) On weekends, we'd watch *Roy Rogers* (King of the Cowboys), *Hopalong Cassidy*, *The Lone Ranger*, and *Sky King*. Family variety shows were popular as well. Ed Sullivan was dominant on Sunday nights, but my favorite was Jackie Gleason, especially when he played Reggie Van Gleason III, a spoiled, rich kid who dressed in white tie and tails and drank shots delivered to him on his model train.

Serious adult shows exposed young people to drama through series like *Playhouse 90*, police capers like *Dragnet*, courtroom dramas like *Perry Mason*, and supernatural ones like *The Twilight Zone*. People began to get their news on TV, and the medium became an immense format for advertisers. Adding a visual connection to the media really amplified pop culture, and all this was before color.

Everyone played outside in those days, no matter what the weather. We lived near the Darby Creek (*Crick* in Philly dialect), and there was a trolley trestle over the creek. That was where we went sledding and climbed trees. Down on the creek, there was a plastic mill that produced records. Once, we went down there and emptied a barrel full of records one at a time like Frisbees into the creek. We were having lots of fun, until we got caught. To use a well-known phrase, I was "scared straight" and never went near that mill again. This experience taught me two valuable lessons: Think about the consequences before you act. And don't just go along with the crowd. You may be surprised where you would wind up.

We had some truly amazing Christmases in that house. Once, a neighbor dressed up as Santa and came over on Christmas Eve to tell us we were the very first house he was visiting. Since Frankie and I shared a bedroom, we stayed up almost all night talking. The next morning, we were showered with bicycles and Western outfits. I'll never forget it.

I attended grade school at Garrettford Elementary. It was very close to our house, only a few blocks away. It was safe to walk to school in those days. I wasn't a very attentive student, daydreaming most of the time. The work seemed so easy.

On March 4, 1954, while my mother and grandmother were shopping in Lit Brothers (a local department store), I tripped and fell headfirst into a showcase. I was rushed to Fitzgerald Mercy Hospital in Lansdowne and was diagnosed with a fractured skull, brain concussion, and muscle impairment in my right eye. I was in the hospital for over a week and missed a lot of school. Ultimately, this event would have a major impact on my life, sometimes positive but mostly not. I will explain in later chapters.

As mentioned previously, my mother loved horses. Well, so did my father—racehorses. My father frequented two racetracks, Garden State in New Jersey and Delaware Park (obviously in Delaware). We would take the train to Delaware Park, a real locomotive. I had no idea how he got me in. He loved to play the ponies. When he won, we splurged. When he lost, it would worry my mother sick. In many ways, he was the eternal optimist, always expecting to win tomorrow. Gambling more than he could afford to lose was a tough lesson for my father, but he did learn from it. Nevertheless, later in life, we enjoyed many trips to the crap tables together, never betting at a level that would break the bank. "You gotta know when to hold 'em and know when to fold 'em."

211 Wilde Avenue

Bob

Frankie

Bob

BROOMALL

In 1955, we moved to a ranch house in Broomall, not very far from Drexel Hill and still in Delaware County. We lived there until 1962 in four different houses. I finished elementary school at Charles H. Russell and later attended Marple Newtown Junior High and Marple Newtown Senior High. My mother continued to work at Wanamaker's in Wynnewood, and my father was selling roofing and siding. Nana and Joe continued to live with us through 1961.

As a result of my skull fracture, I wasn't allowed to play any contact sports that might involve head injury, so I played soccer in the fifth and sixth grades. I was also an avid swimmer and later would participate on the high school swim team. Out of my father's love of baseball, it became my favorite sport. My father would take Frankie and me to Phillies games in the old Connie Mack Stadium. Later in high school, I actually played on the Marple Newtown High School baseball team with Connie Mack's grandson. On occasion, my godfather (Bob Forstburg) and my father would take me with them when they played golf at

Valley Forge Golf Club. They'd let me take a few shots every now and then, and the result was that I fell in love with the game.

My mother's elder brother, my uncle Jack (John Fortune Kane), still lived in Drexel Hill, so we would see his family regularly. Jackie, his eldest son, was a few months older than me, so we would hang out together quite a bit. I adored both my uncle Jack and Joe.

When I was about ten years old, my mother had me audition for a Wanamaker fashion show. I was selected and got my first job at John Wanamaker, never imagining that someday I would become the store's CEO.

In the midfifties, a new TV show premiered in Philadelphia, *Bob Horn's Bandstand*. Local kids were invited to try out and, if selected, dance on the show. It was a very small studio in West Philadelphia at Forty-Sixth and Market Streets. We could get there on the El from Sixty-Ninth Street. In 1956, Bob Horn—who was allegedly taking advantage of some of the teenage girls—was replaced on the show by Dick Clark. Clark made national headlines, and the show became a phenomenon, broadcasting all over the country. Early on in the show, I noticed there were very few couples, so I really worked on learning to dance when I was about thirteen. Girls didn't want to dance with other girls; they wanted to dance with boys, especially if you were a good dancer, and I was.

American Bandstand became the show to watch as soon as you got home from school. Clark developed a format with guest stars (everyone except Elvis), spotlight dances and the introduction of new dance steps, including the hop, the hand jive, the stroll, the cha-cha-cha, the twist, the pony, the fly, the jerk, the locomotion, the swim, the frug, and the watusi. Many of the teen idols were from Philadelphia (Frankie Avalon, Bobby Rydell, and Chubby Checker).

My interest in dancing was really soaring, and my mother would teach me to jitterbug, slow-dance, and even waltz. In 1960 and 1961, I would audition for tickets at the Friday night sock hop at Saint Alice's. June Barbagallo (the girl next door) and Mimi Deerie were my most frequent partners, and we always got tapped and given tickets. Clark was a real taskmaster. Since the show was broadcast live, he was a stickler for the rules. Unless you were on the dance floor, you had to remain in the bleachers, or you were out.

I loved music and dance and also sang in the choir at the Church of Incarnation in Drexel Hill, until my alto voice lost any range, a common occurrence among young men. Nellie (my paternal grandmother) even bought me a guitar. I took lessons for a while but wasn't very good. It made a cool prop.

Another event of some significance in my life happened in 1960 during the presidential race. Both John Kennedy and Richard Nixon came to Broomall to campaign. The Nixons came through in a convertible, waving to the crowd. The week before, John Kennedy came through but got out of his vehicle to have a rally at the Lawrence Park Shopping Center. I didn't have particularly good feelings about Nixon but was enthralled with Kennedy, so I went to the rally and was able to get up close enough to press the flesh with JFK. He was such a fabulous speaker, mesmerized the crowd. It really made an impact on me.

Joe and I really began to bond when I was thirteen. By then, he was on his third car, a 1958 Chevy Impala. It was the hottest car in the county—Continental kit, Hurst four on the floor, 4:11 positraction rear. Just riding shotgun was a thrill.

Joe was always into building models—planes, trains, ships, cars, and platforms. We worked a lot together on a platform for some HO gauge trains he'd given me. He also gave me a .22-caliber bolt-action Springfield rifle and took me to the range to target-practice. Joe was my idol. Any advice he gave me I took seriously. In many ways, he was another person who prompted me to reach for the stars.

In December 1961, Joe married Pat (Knapp), his longtime sweetheart. I was thrilled to be an usher in their wedding. Shortly thereafter, they moved to Miami, where he started engineering school at Embry-Riddle College of Aeronautics.

At about that same time, Nana decided to live with her longtime significant other, Uncle Cam. Cameron Russell was the most generous man I'd ever met. He worked for General Baking Company and had been transferred to Baltimore. In those days they actually delivered bread door-to-door to ensure freshness.

Also in the fall of 1961, Nellie was diagnosed with inoperable cancer. My father was devastated. His mother had been the mainstay of his life, working as a governess to support him after his father abandoned them. She came to live with us until she passed away in March of 1962. I had been in her room, sitting with her, when she collapsed. I picked her up, laid her on the bed, and took her pulse. I knew she was gone. I ran to get my mother, who immediately got Dr. Himmelstein, who lived a few doors away, to come over. He confirmed her death. My father didn't get home for several hours, and hearing the news, he fell apart. He sobbed for days. It was the first time I'd ever seen him cry. The loss of his mother had such an impact on my father that he decided to put our life in Pennsylvania behind us.

Nellie's death made my relationship with my father much stronger. I thought, for him, it was the wake-up call he needed. He became less of a disciplinarian and more of a father who wanted to guide and inspire his children. For me, actually observing my father's vulnerability resonated in a major way. Up to that point, I had never heard him say the words "I love you."

Nana and Cam had decided to retire to Sarasota, where Cam's brother Chick lived. Joe was in Miami, and my father would go to Florida for the spring training baseball season. Sometime that summer, my parents decided to move to Florida. Leaving my friends was hard, but we partied for a few weeks before I left. The last night was a most memorable evening, all the hugging and kissing. I was overwhelmed.

Joe Houck & Elsie "Nana" Houck

2214 Sproul Road

Modeling at Wanamaker's

Frank & Bob

Bob & Pat

Houck Wedding

FLORIDA

My first experience flying was when my mother, brother, and I flew from Philadelphia to Florida—on a prop plane. I think it was a DC-6. There were commercial jets in the air then. We just didn't happen to be on one.

For the first month or so, we lived in a small trailer across from Nana and Cam. My father joined us some time later, and we lived in a rental house near Riverview High School. Unfortunately for all of us, the moving van—with all our worldly possessions—caught on fire in Weeki Wachee, just north of Tampa. Everything was lost—antiques, family heirlooms, all our clothing and furniture, as well as our personal belongings. I was particularly upset about losing my rifle, my train platform, and my letter sweater for baseball. This was a devastating loss for our family. To make matters worse, the moving company deducted loading and freight charges from what little insurance coverage was provided. We were virtually starting over from scratch.

Attending Riverview High School was fun, and for the first time, I actually felt stimulated. I made friends easily, mostly with the other new kids who had transferred in. I had several teachers whom I really liked—Coach Brown, Dr. Marani, Eddie Franklin (who later hired me to work at WFSU, a campus radio station at Florida State University [FSU]), Señor Mosney (who had played basketball at the University of Florida), Coach Pugh, and Mr. Haygood. Other than my brother, my closest friends were Gil McGill, Eddie Schwartz, Jimmy Natherson, Wayne Harris, Mike Cushman, Jeff Bartlett, Bob Sampy, Lester McFawn, and Scott Clarke. There were two girls I played tennis with quite often, Jan Burton and Cathy Harris. Jim Natherson, Wayne Harris, Cathy Harris, and Lester McFawn all did come to FSU. Gilbert had moved from Baltimore to Sarasota. He and I started our own (unauthorized) chapter of his fraternity from Baltimore.

We had lots of fun—beach parties, cruising the town, and just generally hanging out. One time we all swam out to the light tower in Sarasota Bay and mooned the boats returning to dock.

My girlfriend throughout my senior year and freshman year in college was Judy Marx. Her father was a rabbi, and they had relocated to Sarasota from Knoxville, Tennessee. Her family wasn't too excited about us dating. Since she lived in Kensington Park, most of the girls we ran with lived there too—Judy, Carol, and Lindy Rosenbaum and Debbie Hancock. Lindy later edged out my first wife to be named Miss Sarasota in 1968. Gilbert dated Judy Rosenbaum for a while. We all went to prom together with Scott Clarke and his date. I was really crazy about Judy, despite the challenges. She and Gilbert were likely the two smartest kids in our class.

The single most devastating event of our senior year occurred on November 22, 1963. At around two o'clock, Mr. Haygood had us all gather in the auditorium and announced that President Kennedy had been shot. We were devastated. Judy and I ran out into the school parking lot and just stood there, hugging each other and crying our hearts out. He was such a hero to our generation. That weekend, we all stayed at the Sabatinis' house, glued to the TV, watching the funeral.

Trading suburban Philadelphia for the sunny beaches of Sarasota turned out to be very fortunate for me in many ways, even despite the losses and starting anew. The friendships were incredible, the beach parties (day or night) were fabulous and fun, and the climate was conducive to running around half naked when we weren't in school. The other activity that I truly loved was playing golf. When Cam's brother Larry moved to Sarasota, he joined Bobby Jones Golf Club and included me in his membership. Cam gave me an old set of clubs, and I haven't stopped playing since.

Near the end of my senior year, my father told me he didn't have the money to send me to college. He suggested I look for a job with a solid company, where I could work my way up. It sounded a little too much like J. Pierpont Finch in *How to Succeed in Business without Really Trying*. Undeterred, I applied to FSU and got accepted. I still had one major lingering problem—how to pay for it.

When Cam's brother Larry moved to Sarasota, he bought a therapeutic furniture company franchise—Niagara. Larry hired my mother and father. It turned out to be a savior for my parents. They were able to reset their lives and did help me through college.

In the summer of '64, I moved into a garage apartment with my then close friend Wayne Harris, who would later follow me to FSU. I got a job as a lifeguard at a local pool (Sun 'n' Fun); helped coach the swim team, later to become head coach; and joined the ranks of the "bronze gods." The years 1963/64 were a period of highs and lows, fun and frustration, but it was just a stop along the ever-winding road of life.

Sarasota Beach Day

Graduation from Riverview HS

Prom 1964

THE FLORIDA STATE UNIVERSITY

In August of 1964, I boarded a Trailways bus in Sarasota with my friend Jim Natherson and headed for Tallahassee. The ticket was $6. I had a small suitcase with a few shirts, a couple of pairs of slacks, a pair of jeans (white Levi's as I recall), of course the swimsuit I'd been running around in all summer, a pair of Bass Weejuns, and no socks.

When I arrived in Tallahassee, I crossed a threshold that would forever change the path of my life. I had about $400 in cash and had not signed up for a dorm room. When I got to housing, I learned there were no dorm rooms left. Dorms were segregated, male and female. Registration was $150, so I had about $250 left to start on my new adventure. I met some upperclassmen from New York who were looking for a third roommate, so I moved in with them, until I got caught and relocated to approved freshman housing.

As I had mentioned earlier, Eddie Franklin—one of my high school teachers— got me a job at WFSU. I helped build sets, printed signs, and rearranged sets for the next shoot. It didn't pay a lot, but it helped. My meal budget was about $1 per day. Coffee and a doughnut were 15¢, and a three-course meal at the Sweet Shop was 67¢. Didn't leave much for lunch.

Judy had opted to go to the University of Florida in Gainesville, much to the delight of her family, where they hoped she would meet some nice Jewish premed student (which she eventually did). Judy and I were really in love and had tried to stay connected after our freshman year in college, but it just didn't work out. My mother really liked Judy. She felt that she was great for me, and she was right. She challenged me a lot, made me consider opinions and views other than my own. We'd shared a lot together, but as I mentioned, it just wasn't to be.

Gilbert had disappeared, as it turned out, back to Baltimore. Fifty-one years after high school, we tracked him down and had a wonderful reunion with him, Judy and Carol Rosenbaum, Judy (Marx, Boyers) Gee, Eddie Schwartz and his wife, Nancy Sabatini, and my brother, Frank, and his wife, Barbara. It was a fun evening and the beginning of reconnecting with Gil.

During a freshman mixer, I made the most mesmerizing eye contact with a beautiful young lady named Suzanne. For me, it was love at first sight. We dated off and on during my freshman year. I even went to Miami to meet her family between my freshman and sophomore years after Judy and I had broken up. But she never had the same feelings for me.

My academic performance as a freshman was lackluster at best, pretty much straight Cs. During freshman orientation, the speaker suggested that only one-third of the freshman class would actually graduate from FSU. Sure enough, my two friends on either side of me did not graduate from FSU, although both did eventually get their degrees. During my sophomore year, I got more serious and even made the dean's list.

I wanted eventually to go to law school and study corporate law, but after taking two undergraduate law courses and getting Cs, I decided I didn't have the aptitude or the attitude for practicing law, so I focused on marketing and business management. Outside the College of Business, I really enjoyed political science, humanities, economics, and statistics. However, once I decided on business, it became 100 percent my focus. I even made the dean's list twice during my last two years.

During my junior year, I joined a business fraternity, Delta Sigma Pi. I was very active and became good friends with Dennis BeMent. Dennis had actually gone to Sarasota High School, and his father (Gene) owned a restaurant in Sarasota. In my senior year, Dennis and I roomed together. We were even each other's best man. We remain great friends to this day.

We were on the trimester system for my first three years, so I would go to school from late August until mid-April and then return to Sarasota to lifeguard and coach. My brother, Frank, also had gotten a job as a lifeguard at Siesta Beach. We certainly enjoyed our "bronze god" status.

During that time, at a party full of lifeguards at my brother's place on Siesta Key, I met Jinx. She was four years younger than me, cute, outgoing, athletic, and generally fun to be with. At the time, she seemed mature for her age. We began dating, and I would see her when I came to Sarasota from school.

In the summer of 1967, I decided to get a job doing construction work and ended up working in a plant that made ready-mix cement and concrete block.

Many of the houses in Florida in those days were concrete block construction. The job paid well, and I got time and a half for overtime and double pay for over sixty hours. But the work was grueling. I was probably in the best physical condition of my young life. Unfortunately, I was injured and hospitalized with a huge hematoma on my right thigh and groin.

When I got out of the hospital, Jinx had convinced both me and her parents that I should stay with them until I returned to school. My parents were in Indiana, working home shows for Niagara. In retrospect, I supposed that sealed the bond between Jinx and me, at least for a while.

In September of that year, I came to Sarasota to see my parents for my birthday. To my absolute surprise, they presented me with a combination birthday and graduation gift—a brand-new 1967 Volkswagen Beetle. I was overjoyed.

Back in Tallahassee, I had gotten a job as a bartender at the local Elks club. It was the only place in Leon County where you could buy liquor across the bar. Everyone who was anyone was an Elk. The pay was okay, the tips were fabulous, and they fed me for free. It did put a damper on my social life though.

My senior year was momentous. As I tell students today when I guest-lecture, "From 1964 to 1968, we went from panty raids to protests." College students all across the nation were protesting our involvement in the Vietnam War. Boomers were a vocal generation. That movement started a culture of questioning the government's positions on many issues but none larger than the war in Vietnam. I had tried to enlist in the reserves but kept failing the physicals because of my eye impairment. When I finally did get drafted, I failed that physical too because of the muscle impairment in my right eye.

During my senior year, I had two professors who took an interest in me, Dr. Dan Voich (management) and Dr. John Kerr (marketing). Both later became the chairs of their respective departments. In different ways, they each challenged me to strive to reach my full potential, their way of telling me to reach for the stars. In 2010, when I was inducted into the FSU College of Business Hall of Fame, I had the great privilege of thanking Dr. Voich publicly at the induction ceremony.

In April of 1968, shortly after a fraternity meeting, we heard that Dr. Martin Luther King had been assassinated in Memphis. Dr. King was idolized on college campuses. How anyone could disagree with his peaceful approach to equality for all was then and is still today mind boggling. It was a terrible night, and for the next few days in Tallahassee, there were riots and looting everywhere. Strangely for me, a few days later, I would find myself in Atlanta, interviewing at Rich's, the day of Dr. King's funeral. I got the job. Just two months later, Robert F. Kennedy would be assassinated in California on the night before my graduation. In a period of four years and seven months, three of the most iconic leaders of the American landscape were assassinated. What a tragedy!

I had a truly amazing four years at FSU. I enjoyed great sports events, homecomings, fraternity parties, and a stimulating environment for learning. It was when I first realized I could be whatever I wanted to be.

1966 Sophomore Year

1968 Senior Year

Graduation Day 1968

June 15, 1968

THE BIG GREEN *R*

Four significant things happened in my life in June of 1968. First, I graduated from FSU with a bachelor of science degree in business management and marketing. Second, nine days later on June 15, 1968, in Sarasota, Florida, I married Jinx at Saint Boniface Church on Siesta Key. Third, after a brief honeymoon in Fort Lauderdale, we moved to Atlanta, Georgia. And fourth, I began to pursue my career dreams (following in my mother's footsteps in retailing) with Rich's. "The big green *R*" was my description of their logo.

I started as a junior executive trainee (JET). There were about thirty of us in my training class. I was placed as a junior assistant buyer, much to my surprise, in handbags. The handbag buyer was a hotshot named Terry Barkin. He was single at the time and lived with his mother, so he was quite the workaholic. We developed an odd relationship. At work, he was demanding and often downright demeaning. Outside work, he was fun to be with. We'd go to ball games together and watch the Braves win and the Falcons lose. Occasionally, we'd eat together, especially if we were going to branch stores in the evening. I put in long hours merchandising the sales floor of the downtown store, checking in merchandise in the receiving area, and working in the stockroom.

I made friends with some of my fellow JETs, most of whom were females— Marcia McCord, B. J. (Betty Jean) Sattler, Janet Niles (who went to FSU), and Linda Hedgepeth, who lived in our apartment complex. Unfortunately, some of these friendships preyed on Jinx's insecurities and definitely put a strain on our marriage. We did make friends with some of our neighbors—Richard and Glenda Robinson and Hume and Ann Cole. Hume was a local golf pro, and Richard (who was in the army at the time) and I could usually be found at Hume's golf course when we had the time.

Early in 1969, Terry was promoted to divisional merchandise manager (DMM) of shoes, in several ways a blessing for my career. With a new buyer— Dick Greene, who had been with Macy's—I was able to develop a relationship with the general merchandise manager, Jay Salzman. Jay really mentored me while Dick gave me my first real merchandising experiences. Dick taught me how to edit and select; spot trends; test, reorder, and clear; and analyze the business in terms of rates of sale and weeks of supply. Dick (through Jay) even arranged to take me on my first buying trip to New York in 1969.

That was such an eye-opening experience for me, meeting the key suppliers, looking at the lines for future delivery, and being part of the selection process. I learned so much that week. I would be forever grateful to these two men, who really mentored me and positioned my career. Perhaps the single most important occurrence of that trip was meeting the wonderful Larry Diamond. Larry was the sales manager of his family business, Markay. We did a terrific business with them, and they were nice people to boot.

Jinx had gone to work for a dentist, but things didn't work out, so she applied for a job at the Rich's store in Greenbrier, near our apartment. She did well, working her way up from the sales floor to be a department manager, but her ultimate goal was to become a mother, not have a career in retailing.

My parents were now spending a lot of their time with their friends, the Coudriets. My father met Regis when they were job searching, and both came to work for my uncle Larry at Niagara. They were inseparable. They loved going fishing together. Much to my father's joy (and dismay), in 1970, my mother broke the world record for boating a 190-pound tarpon in Boca Grande Pass.

Dick Greene left the company and was replaced by a gentleman named Tom Sebring. After some overlap with Tom, I was told by Jay Salzman I'd be made the buyer of ladies' fashion accessories after a short overlap with the existing buyer, Gertrude Church. Mrs. Church had been at Rich's for forty-one years and did not want to retire, nor did she wish to be replaced by a young "whippersnapper Yankee." She did everything she could to make my life miserable for the six-week overlap, but in the end, she was forced to retire. The last thing she said to me was "Sonny, just remember, what you don't buy is every bit as important as what you do buy," reinforcing the disciplines Dick Greene had taught me.

Now here I was in 1971, two and a half years out of college, running my own business; and boy, did I think I was a hotshot. Bernd Schaechter took me to dinner at Chris's Cellar in New York to celebrate my promotion. On the way out of the restaurant after a few twelve-year-old Bell's scotches and a Churchill cigar hanging out of my mouth, I ran smack dab into Joel Goldberg, the president of Rich's. I must've looked like I'd just been taken to the cleaners.

The rest of the JETs in my class were assistant buyers or department managers. Fashion accessories included gloves, scarves, handkerchiefs, umbrellas, rainwear, hats, shawls, belts, and sunglasses. Fashion sunglasses were a new main-floor category, so it added a lot of business. Jay Salzman had guided me to put the lion's share of my open-to-buy with a company named Renauld, a division of Foster Grant. This began a lifelong friendship with Tom Easton, the president of Renauld, and Dick Fields, who really knew how to build and service a business. Easton recognized early that there was a significant opportunity in the upscale sunglass business. And with his cosmetics background, he really understood marketing at point of sale to engage the customer to try on the glasses. The product was good, the promotion was sensational, the execution was terrific, and the sales exploded, making me buyer of the year.

There were numerous other hot categories—dome umbrellas, telescopic and folding umbrellas, knit hat and scarf sets, Isotoner gloves, and tube tops. Of course, each year, you have to improve on last year's performance.

When I became a buyer, we moved from our second apartment to a home in Stone Mountain. We found a nice split-level home in a new neighborhood. We were really excited. My commute was a little longer but not bad. I joined a golf club (Snapfinger Woods) and made several new friends there. We played golf together; went camping up near Buford Dam, where they filmed the movie *Deliverance*, starring Burt Reynolds; and enjoyed each other. During that time, Jinx seemed more settled and generally much happier. We agreed it was about time to start a family. Christopher Patrick Mang came into the world at Northside Hospital in Atlanta on March 16, 1973.

Jinx was very anxious as she was two weeks beyond her delivery date. We went to the hospital for her to be induced and found out she was already in labor. After some complications with her epidural, things were corrected, and Chris was delivered naturally at around four in the afternoon. This was certainly the most joyous moment in my life up to that point and would only be equaled with the births of my two incredible daughters years later.

That spring, I became a Mason. I also attended my first masters tournament, won by Tommy Aaron, a native Georgian. On the career front, I had developed an excellent reputation in the market, so a few other companies were approaching me. I liked Rich's but was only making $12,000 a year. Coincidently, my mentor Jay Salzman was leaving and going to Stix, Baer & Fuller in Saint Louis. Bernd Schaechter, with whom I had developed a great relationship when I was an assistant buyer, had recommended me to Gimbels in Philadelphia to buy handbags. I consulted with Larry Diamond, who already knew I was the number 1 candidate. They offered me $18,000 a year, which of course was a major incentive. Additionally, I didn't feel like my career was going anywhere at Rich's. Also, I was sure that at some point in the future Terry would become my boss again. Oddly, Terry and I became close friends years later, to be discussed in another chapter.

1520 Walnut Ridge Court

Shakin' not Stirred

Christopher Patrick Mang
March 16, 1973

Reeling in the Tarpon

World Record Tarpon
Caught on 50lb test

FULL CIRCLE

Chris was only a few months old when I made the decision to accept the Gimbels offer and about six months old when we relocated. We found a house in suburban New Jersey, near the Lindenwold train station, so I would have an easy commute both into New York and Philadelphia. The community was Laurel Springs. We made friends with some neighbors (Frank and Linda Scioli) who would again be our neighbors in Miami.

My boss at Gimbels was a real character (Murray Goldstein) but not a very good merchant. He was very lucky to have had some very talented buyers. There were a lot of management changes upon my arrival. A top merchant, Manny Rosenberg from Filene's in Boston, came in as president. As expected, he immediately began to build his team. Fortunately for me, he took an instant interest in me probably because my business was booming and because I had come from Rich's, a store he was quite familiar with. As Manny made changes, he brought in some great people. In a few cases, they became very dear friends.

At the end of my first year, Manny decided to expand my exposure to get some apparel experience and appointed me as the blouse buyer. I heard that Sue Nodine, who had been the handbag buyer at Filene's, was replacing me. I made a call to my trusted friend Larry Diamond to attempt to confirm the rumors. As usual, he had all the skinny. Sue did replace me and became one of the most important people in my life—a wonderful friend, a classy lady, and a phenomenal dance partner. She won so many ballroom dance competitions that she didn't have enough room to display them.

A small group of us went to coffee and to lunch together almost every day— Joyce Mantyla, also from Filene's and an apparel buyer at the time; Fran Ferrar, the hosiery buyer; Jean Peters, the jewelry buyer; and Howard Shub, the notions buyer. Sue and I remained the closest of friends throughout her life. Shortly before her death, I took Sue on a marvelous trip to France. We were in Paris on Bastille Day; took a barge through the Burgundy region of France, visiting chateaus and wineries; and even did a hot-air balloon ride over a chateau and vineyard. We finished the trip in Nice, where we toured the Rothschild estate and ate at all the finest restaurants. Sue had a relapse of ovarian cancer, which took her life in 2009. She was a most important influence and the dearest friend. I loved spending time with her. I continue to be amazed at the impact women have had on my entire life's journey.

7 Constitution Road

Mang Style

3 Generation of Mang Men

Chris' Christening St. Bonafice

Gimbels Gang

UP, UP, AND AWAY

Early in 1975, J. L. Tonner—the highly regarded recruiter for Federated Department Stores (FDS)—contacted me. Federated owned the most venerable portfolio of companies in the United States: Bloomingdale's, Burdines, Abraham & Straus (A&S), Filene's, Lazarus, Shillito's, Rike's, Bullock's, Foley's, and Sanger-Harris, to mention a few. They had actually acquired Rich's as well. JL and I really connected. She immediately wanted to know in which companies I might be interested and why. We talked about Bloomingdale's, Burdines, and Bullock's mostly, and then she asked what it would take for me to make a change. I immediately said, "Career growth."

Within two weeks, she had me interviewing with Mel Jacobs, the president of Burdines; and a month later, they offered me a job buying several departments in the junior division. I was elated with the prospect of being back in Florida with a company that had aggressive growth plans.

Jinx, Chris, and I made the move to Miami in the summer of 1975. I had decided to live in an apartment for a few months until we sold our house in

New Jersey, so we found a nice two-bedroom rental right behind Burdines' Dadeland store. We actually moved from New Jersey to Miami on the auto train.

Our first year was a very mixed bag. It was lots of fun being in the Sun 'n' Fun capital of the world (according to the famous Jackie Gleason), but my job was very stressful. I didn't have a good relationship with my boss, Gwen Love. And I was constantly going to New York because of all the different categories I was responsible for.

On the fun side of the equation, I bought a boat from a friend of my father's, so we had great weekend getaways on the boat. Sometimes I'd go deep-sea fishing; other times, we'd water-ski in Biscayne Bay. Sometimes we'd just anchor off Elliott Key.

Water-skiing resulted in the scariest moment of my entire life. As a friend of mine, Ed Pruitt, was running the boat and I was water-skiing, Chris went overboard without a life preserver on. He was only a little over two but had learned to swim when he was about a year old. When I got back in the boat, I said, "Where's Chris?" And we realized he'd fallen overboard. I could see his head bobbing in the distance. I grabbed the controls and sped full throttle to him. My lifeguard instincts kicked in, so I dived in the water and lifted him to be sure he was breathing.

When we got back in the boat, Chris was fine. He said he'd swallowed a little water was all. I was furious with Jinx and Marilyn Pruitt; neither of them had seen Chris fall out of the boat. Shortly after that incident, I sold the boat.

Subsequent boating trips with Ed Pruitt were equally frightening. At one point, the engine on his boat caught on fire after a series of errors, including a fire extinguisher that didn't work. The boat, with all my fishing and scuba gear, burned to the waterline while I was getting Chris and Ed's son, Eddie, to safety. Years later, a friend of mine nicknamed Ed "Crash Pruitt" based on a few other Pruitt mishaps.

Toward the end of my first year, I was very frustrated with my job and perhaps too vocal about it. I was summoned to Mel Jacobs's office, where he sternly encouraged me to focus on the job at hand and not to be so concerned with my career path. That conversation, as difficult as it was for me to hear, may well have been one of the defining points in my career. I was off track, and Mel put me back on track.

A few months later, I was appointed as a divisional merchandise manager in the Dadeland store. I was there for a little over a year and reported to a regional store manager named George Corrigan (who in later years became mayor of Coral Gables). George was a very smart executive with a big-picture focus. He taught me everything I know about store operations, and I give him credit for moving my career along.

When I first got to Dadeland, I thought, *If these stores knew what they were doing, we'd do a lot more business.*

Later, I began to think, *If our merchants knew what they were doing, we'd do a lot more business.* Then I realized that Mel's vision of teaching his high-potential executives to think big was really the key to my career path. Mel, who was very hard to get to know, challenged me on every front but also supported my initiatives. He was a great merchant who went on to become vice chairman of Federated and later worked for Arnold Aronson, running Saks Fifth Avenue. Mel died young at age sixty-seven. The last time I saw him, he was CEO of

Saks, and I was president of Woodies and Wanamaker's, reporting then to Arnold Aronson. Mel and I sat together at the National Retail Federation (NRF) conference.

Dennis Bookshester, the general merchandise manager (GMM) of the fashion store, was terrific. He would later become president of Sibley's in Rochester, New York. John Burden, who became president of Burdines, was great to work with. He had a great sense of humor. Later, he would become CEO of Abraham & Straus, vice chairman of Federated, and ultimately CEO of Federated. When I was promoted to divisional merchandise manager of fashion accessories, I reported to Herb Ross, who was now at the GMM level. Herb (a.k.a. Herbie) was incredibly supportive and absolutely fun to work with. He had been the hosiery buyer and the divisional merchandise manager (my new job). The best advice I got from Herb was "We already know you're a great merchant. Now show us you're a great leader." We made some fabulous trips together.

Being back in Florida meant I would see more of my parents. Years prior, they made an unannounced visit in Atlanta that Jinx handled poorly, so my father refused to visit us and didn't for seven years, until we moved back to Florida. My parents had been living in a mobile home in the winter and traveled during the summer for Niagara. As my folks got back on their feet financially, they moved into a condo on Phillippi Creek, bought a boat, and spent a lot of time with their friends Regis and Jesse Coudriet fishing and traveling with Niagara.

In 1978, ten years after my graduation from FSU, I felt on top of the world in my career pursuits. It was a great time on a number of fronts.

Music and pop culture were having a major impact on the retail business, enabling us to spot trends quickly and with some assurance. Things like engineered prints, platform shoes, tight-fitting jeans, and a new wave of designers: Ralph Lauren, Calvin Klein, Perry Ellis, Donna Karan, Albert and Pearl Nipon, Liz Claiborne, Bill Blass, and Halston hitting their stride. Also, there was the wave of successful international designers setting the fashion stage: Christian Dior, Yves Saint Laurent, Karl Lagerfeld, Armani, Versace, Fendi, Gucci, Cartier, and Missoni, to name a few. But most important was the emergence of women in the workforce, driving a major push to career dressing.

At Burdines under Mel's leadership, we were closing old downtown stores and replacing them with upscale brand-new units in the best locations—Boca Town Center, Fort Lauderdale Galleria, and West Palm Beach. We were also expanding into the west coast of Florida and taking advantage of the population growth in the state. We all felt like we'd hit the jackpot, and we had.

During my first market trip to Europe with Herb, we ran into Ralph Destino, then president of Cartier. He invited us to a Cartier party that would introduce their new Santos watch dedicated to famous aviators. As it turned out, Herb and I were the only two Americans to attend. The party began at 10:30 p.m., and there were 738 people in attendance. It was one of the wildest and craziest nights of my life. It was like the Academy Awards. All the famous and wealthy Parisians were there. Cartier flew in nine famous aviators to kick off the party and presented each with a Santos watch. They served lobster thermidor and Moët champagne, and the gala went on past three in the morning.

A gentleman at our table offered us a ride back to Paris as the event was hosted at Le Bourget (the French national air museum). That was when things got really crazy. On the way back into Paris, our newfound friend asked us if we'd like to go to Regine's for a nightcap. Regine was famous for her work in the French resistance in WWII. Of course, we said yes. On the way, our friend—while circling around the Arc de Triomphe—rear-ended the car in front of us. There was no damage to his Jaguar, but he wrote a check to the guy he hit, and off we went to Regine's. Upon arrival, Regine herself met us at the door and took us to a private room where another magnum of Moët awaited.

I wasn't used to pulling all-nighters, and so at about five o'clock, we left, suddenly realizing we had a buyers' meeting in the morning, and then we were going to the Prêt-à-Porter (the designer fair). We met with the buyers for breakfast at seven thirty and headed to the Prêt at around nine, and on the verge of passing out, I took a cab back to the hotel and slept until dinner that night.

Traveling with Herbie was one adventure after another. Herb Ross was a delight. He later became president of Rike's, Shillito's, Lazarus, and later the Bon-Ton.

I was able to maintain many of my friendships in the market when I was in Dadeland and rekindle some of them when I became the accessories divisional manager. In Dadeland, I met a woman who would become in many ways the backbone of my success, Bert Adamo. Bert had worked in the junior area, and I wanted her to manage our fine jewelry department. She accepted and did a superb job. This would begin an incredible relationship.

Bert introduced me to Larry Dunn, a former Vietnam helicopter pilot who was then flying for Eastern Air Lines. Larry offered to teach me to fly. I soloed after only seven hours. He really put me through the ropes. Once, he put me in a power-on stall tailspin and laughed while I tried to right the aircraft.

I loved flying and spent hours flying with Dave Dyer, a good friend who later would become CEO of Lands' End and Home Shopping Network and president of Tommy Hilfiger. Dave did very well. Dave and I would fly from Miami down to Key West, have lunch, and fly back. On one trip, he let Chris—who was about seven—take the controls. Bill Lechtner, another great friend, also flew, and we spent some time in the air together.

Larry Diamond always stayed in touch with me, virtually calling me weekly just to see how I was doing. Of course, I would see Dick Fields when he came to town and Bernd Schaechter. Bob Melzer and I had become great friends too. I also stayed in touch with Terry Barkin, who was still with Rich's and, as I had suspected, was now the GMM of men's, children's, cosmetics, shoes, lingerie, and accessories.

Through Dick Fields, I was introduced to Bert Perez, who would become one of my dearest lifelong friends. Bert was hired by Dick to run the sales and service operations at Renauld. Bert was born in Cuba, went to military school in the United States, and was exiled to Spain with his family when the Castros took over their plantation. Once we met, it was an instant friendship. We just truly enjoyed each other's company.

During one of the trips they made to Miami, they rented a house on Key Biscayne. Dick (a lifelong Boston Bruins fan and season ticket holder) invited me over to play tennis very early in the morning. When I showed up wearing a Philadelphia Flyers jersey, Bert couldn't stop laughing. Dick, who was a better tennis player than me, was so distracted by the jersey that he lost the match. Earlier in my career, Dick had invited me to Boston for one of the Stanley Cup final games between the Bruins and Flyers. When André "Moose" DuPont scored an overtime goal to win the game (and ultimately take the cup), Dick was beside himself, and I was afraid that someone in the Boston Garden might recognize me as a Flyers fan. Whenever I was in New York, we always got together for dinner somewhere special.

In the late '70s, the music rage had become disco, and Miami seemed like the disco capital of the world. Even the Bee Gees lived on Miami Beach. What a great time to be in Miami, especially given my history and love for music and dance.

After only two years as a divisional merchandise manager, I was promoted to vice president of accessories and shoes, coincidently on the same day as Bob Wechsler was made VP of junior's and children's. We were both thrilled and celebrated with each other over a special dinner with our wives.

The most important thing I'd learned about shoes was that you had to own depth of key sizes. Ironically, Rich's had the most successful business in Federated. So I called Terry, and he invited me to come up to Atlanta for a few days, reprise a couple of branch store trips, and study Rich's business. It was quite extraordinary to me that, after having such an acrimonious relationship when I was his assistant, we could be working together again. He was instrumental in helping me develop a solid business strategy for the Burdines shoe business, resulting in a 41 percent increase in sales and the best performance in Federated.

By this point, I had also built a strong team of buyers in fashion accessories. Bert Adamo was now racking up numbers in luggage and sunglasses that were phenomenal. Amy Park, who had come to us from A&S, had a stellar performance as the hosiery buyer. I had split handbags in two, achieving great results with Leslie Palmer in the designer and more upscale business and Penny Berg running the mainstream business. I had also split the jewelry area, putting Sue Kirchner in the key growth segment and keeping the wonderful Jo Angelica in the core area. My fashion accessories buyer, Marty Davis, was an absolute delight. She was from Mendenhall, Mississippi, and a true southerner. Like Bert Adamo, her work ethic was unbelievable, and she always had a smile on her face.

There was a real opportunity to grow the semiprecious jewelry business with gold-plated silver jewelry, silver jewelry, and gold-filled jewelry. This was the area for which Sue Kirchner was responsible. Once again, I called on Dick Fields to help. He had gone to work for a Chicago jewelry company named Princess Pride, run by a gentleman named Gary Solomon. They owned the name Milano, so we launched it at Burdines. It was a solid success.

I stayed friendly with Gary throughout the '80s but later lost touch. During the spring of 1981, Gary invited me to join him and play in the Doral pro-am. Subsequently, he invited me to play there until 1990. In 1984, we had the spectacular opportunity to play with the greatest golfer of all time, Jack Nicklaus. I was a nervous wreck. My parents even came down to see me play. Jack couldn't have been nicer. What a great ambassador for the marvelous game of golf and a thrill of a lifetime for me.

I had promoted Amy Smithes, who also had a legendary work ethic, to divisional merchandise manager of shoes. Managing her shoe team was a challenge, but she rose to the occasion. One thing I was certain of was that every one of these people, all women, had a great eye for product.

Life was great for the most part. I was uncomfortable with the GMM I was reporting to, but I was exhilarated with the results, the concepts I'd put in place, and life in general. I was running a lot. Chris would follow me on his bicycle. It was such a wonderful and fulfilling bonding experience.

In 1980, Jinx became pregnant and would deliver Lauren Elise Mang into the world on April 22, 1981 (now Earth Day) at Baptist Hospital in Miami, just down the road from Burdines' Dadeland store, where I had worked in 1977. I was truly delighted—a son and a lovely daughter. I felt we were now the perfect family. However, things don't always work out the way you expect them to.

I was now being courted by John Wanamaker to come in at the general merchandise manager level and run cosmetics, intimate apparel, fashion accessories, shoes, coats, dresses, and women's apparel. Wow, John Wanamaker, where I had been a ten-year-old model.

My going-away party was quite the blast. I actually wore a Superman outfit. The girls who worked for me hired a belly dancer, and everyone took lots of pictures of all the fun and frolicking. Jinx even seemed to have a good time. That party, and particularly those pictures, would come back to haunt me just two years later in a courtroom in Media, Pennsylvania.

Showing off my boat

Indian Guides

Cowboy Chris

Key West 1978

Flying the plane

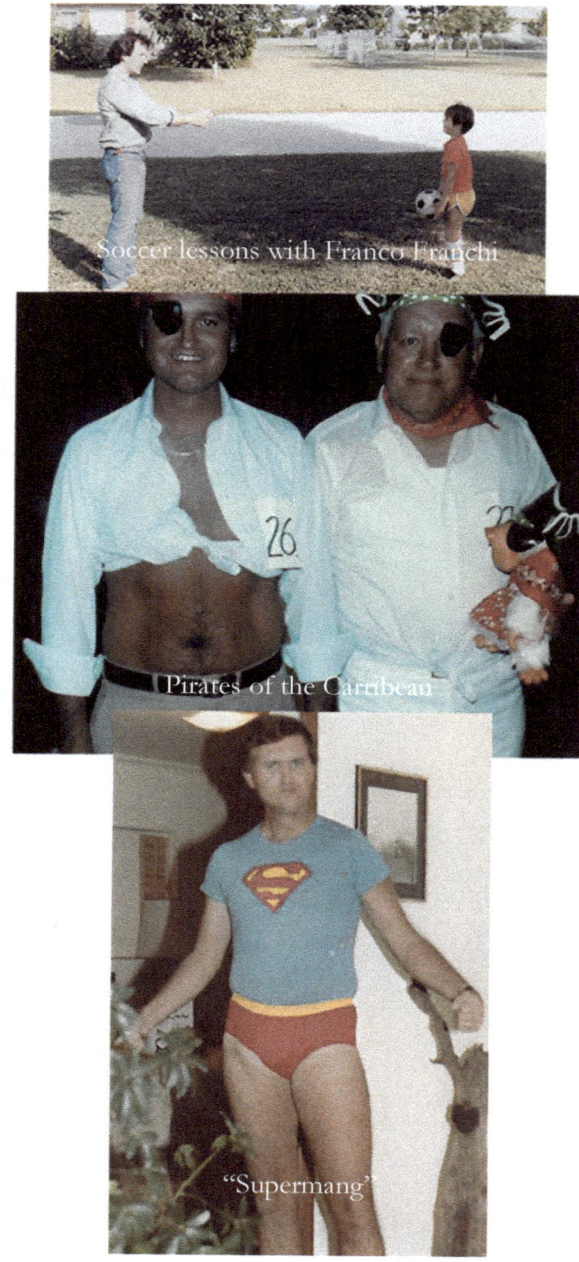

Soccer lessons with Franco Franchi

Pirates of the Carribean

"Supermang"

RETURNING TO MY PHILADELPHIA ROOTS

Tom Easton was friendly with Dick Hauser, who had been the president of Neiman Marcus and the Broadway before being named CEO of Wanamaker's. Over a period of a couple of months, I had several interviews with the senior management group at John Wanamaker. They offered me the job with a starting salary 67 percent more than I was making at Burdines and added a contract with bonus opportunity. My start date was August 1, 1981.

The company set me up in temporary housing just off the Benjamin Franklin Parkway and not far from the store. I was there for about three months before I moved the whole family. We found my dream home, actually very close to where I had gone to high school in Newtown Square. The house was a two-story colonial set on a hill and right across the street from the famous Aronimink Golf Club, where they had played the 1962 PGA Championship when I was in high school.

During my first week at Wanamaker's, I met two people who had worked with my mother and remembered me as a child. Harriet Vaughn was now the executive assistant to Ted Kutzer, the head of stores (I used to roller-skate with her daughter Charla at Chez Vous). And Bill Christine still worked in Big Ticket and remembered that his daughter and I had modeled together in 1955. He even still had a picture of us. I became very friendly with Bill, often playing golf together.

Running five divisions, at this level, demanded a much different skill set than my previous position at Burdines. I knew I'd have to really share my vision and develop long-term strategies as well as tactical plans to grow the business. I knew that our assortments would have to be built around customer preference and demand. Also, our marketing would need to be multimedia, then including newspapers, magazines (direct mail), and broadcast (both radio and TV).

I also recognized that I would need a new team who understood my vision. I persuaded Kai Frost (the former president of Gimbels and now senior VP of marketing at JW) to bring Joyce Mantyla in to run public relations. I was able to entice Bert Adamo to buy fine jewelry and Sue Kirchner to come to JW to buy bras. I was very fortunate to be able to hire Muriel Gonzalez away from Bloomingdale's to run our cosmetics business. And to top it off, I got Sue Nodine to leave CBS and buy handbags. These women made me look like a genius. My business skyrocketed, and I got a lot of attention both in the market and from Carter Hawley Hale (CHH), the owners of the company.

Unfortunately, Jinx did not adapt well at all to the move. Furthermore, my attempts to include her more in my business life backfired. Her anxiety and frustration grew, and her insecurity manifested itself in untrue accusations regarding my fidelity. As this behavior mounted, I decided to get some legal advice regarding the ramifications of a separation. Unfortunately, that fueled Jinx's anxiety and insecurity to the brink. In short order, she hired an attorney who directed her to sue me for abandonment and lack of support and accuse me of infidelity and even had a constable serve me as well as Dick Hauser, my boss, a subpoena in our offices.

In October 1982, Lauren was just eighteen months old, and Chris was nine and a half. I had committed to support Jinx and my children but wanted joint custody. At the advice of her attorney, she fought against this tooth and nail. Fortunately, I took Chris to see a therapist who volunteered to testify that I should have primary custody. The ensuing months were terribly stressful. Jinx's attorney was extremely aggressive and dragged me to court multiple times. Ultimately, I would prevail on the custody front. When we settled, I gave her 100 percent of our assets (primarily the house in Newtown Square) and about 50 percent of my pay at the time for nine years. Fortunately for me, shortly after my divorce, I got a raise and a bonus for my performance, putting me on more certain financial footing.

Robert B. Mang
Sr. Vice President John Wanamaker

Frank Sr. & Chris

Chris & Lauren

Bob, Lauren & Chris

Bob & Lauren

Muriel, Bob and Bert

At the Helm of Tiburon

Skiing Copper Mountain

Chris, as Joseph, in Joseph and the Amazing
Technicolor Dream Coat

Bob & Lauren

AGONY TO ECSTASY

In November of 1982, after I had filed the separation papers, the company sent me to Japan with a team of people to put together a fashion "fortnight" for Wanamaker's. On the return to Philadelphia, we had a layover in Honolulu. This would begin a new and most significant chapter in my life.

The Japanese fortnight would be the first time an American department store would showcase Japanese designers and fashions. We already had strong relationships with numerous Japanese suppliers—Seiko watches, Shiseido cosmetics, and Mikimoto pearls, to name a few. Designers like Kenzo, Yamaguchi, Hanae Mori, and Rae Watanabe were getting huge notoriety; and the prospect of selling fine silks, kimonos, *happi* coats, pearls, and other key items was most appetizing. It was an ambitious project but extremely exciting.

On that trip, I really got to know our fashion coordinator, Hilda Lewis. Her insights were spot on, and she wowed not only the Japanese suppliers but me as well. The rest of the team included Bert Adamo, Carolyn Shea (the accessories DMM), and Muriel Gonzalez, who was an absolute, upbeat, positive bundle of energy. We made several trips putting that fortnight together.

Shortly after the November trip, Bert Adamo came to me with an idea. She had talked the local distributor of Seiko, who had connections in the music business, into sponsoring an event at the orchestra's Academy of Music to promote the fortnight. In short order, they put together a truly special evening. Peter Nero conducted the Philly Pops Orchestra. The velvet-voiced Mel Tormé was the featured star. We even had Tug McGraw (a famous relief pitcher for the NY Mets and Philadelphia Phillies) read "The Night before Christmas." Bert and I sat with Sammy Cahn (the famous Academy Award–winning songwriter of Frank Sinatra's many hits). The event was a smashing success.

In Tokyo, we all stayed at the Okura Hotel, a famous landmark. Then we visited Osaka (where we purchased Sanyo rainwear); the beautiful city of Kyoto, where we visited all the amazing Shinto shrines and bought pearls; and even Hiroshima. By now, after two trips to Japan, I was more than just smitten with Hilda. She not only had a great eye for fashion, an engaging personality, and a great sense of humor but she also carried herself with beauty and dignity. There was one major problem; she was married to a navy pilot who was often off on deployment, and he was married to the navy. She really struggled with their marriage.

In the fall of 1983, we pulled our fashion event off to great fanfare. Numerous Japanese dignitaries attended, as well as local politicians and leaders. Hanae Mori was the featured designer. Even our retail friends from New York came to Philadelphia to attend the event.

The following year, we did an Italian fortnight. Italy had been done before, but nevertheless, our event was a booming success. By now, Chris was living with me full time in a townhouse in Downtown Philadelphia. Jinx had moved to Chesterbrook, near Valley Forge. Chris attended Friends Select in Downtown Philly, just a few blocks from Wanamaker's. Lauren attended Valley Forge Country Day School, but I had her every other weekend and all summer.

On weekends when I could and the weather was agreeable, I'd get away to Stamford, Connecticut, and go boating with Bert and Dee Perez. There were a number of these trips over the years, and it is hard to separate them now. We always had a blast. Dee and I loved to dance and sometimes would dance on the back of the boat until our feet were rubbed raw. On one night, we decided to go serenade Neil Sedaka's boat, also moored at Yacht Haven West, singing "Breakin' Up Is Hard to Do." Much to our surprise, he was on the boat.

My relationship with Hilda was always a bit rocky. She carried a lot of guilt regarding her marriage. When her husband was sent to the Naval War College in Rhode Island, we separated, and she attempted to put her marriage back together. I saw her once during that period when she frantically called me because Richard was on deployment, and Kristen, her niece, was not expected to live through the night as she had a severe asthma attack. Chris and I drove to Newport, Rhode Island (about six hours from Philadelphia), to be with her in this overwhelming time of need. That trip likely opened Hilda's eyes as, a few months later, she was back in Philadelphia to stay.

In 1985, there was a lot going on at Wanamaker's and at Carter Hawley Hale stores (which owned a number of companies). The Limited stores, owned by Les Wexner, had initiated a hostile takeover attempt for CHH to acquire

Neiman Marcus. While the attempt was unsuccessful, it crippled CHH, which was forced to bring in another investor, General Cinema, which did takeover Neiman and Bergdorf Goodman. CHH sold Thalhimers to the May Company and the Waldenbooks and Holt Renfrew (two Canadian companies) to other buyers. Surprisingly, Wanamaker's was retained. That would all change in short order.

While all this was going on, Dick Hauser was replaced by Dick Boje, another CHH executive who had run Weinstock's, one of the California divisions that was going to be consolidated into the Emporium in San Francisco. Hilda had been rehired at JW to be the couture buyer. I was informed of Hauser's departure when I was in Scandinavia, preparing for our next fortnight. I was immediately summoned home.

Dick Boje and I didn't hit it off at the start. Fortunately for me, my performance was carrying the company. I was very concerned about Wanamaker's and my future. I actually began to develop a business plan to start my own series of highend fashion jewelry stores in the event things didn't work out. Career-wise, 1985 was unspectacular, but my personal life seemed great in the latter part of 1984 and into 1985—ski trips with Hilda and Chris, Hilda and I boating with Bert and Dee Perez, and trips to Europe.

On one such trip, Chris came along, and we covered a lot of ground in Italy and Switzerland. As the result of a wildcat Italian workers' strike, we took a train from Milan to Zurich through the snowcapped Alps with Bert Adamo to buy watches. During that trip, we actually found a company named Swatch and were the first American store to buy the product.

There was so much change in the department store business in the mideighties— mergers, acquisitions, and companies closing (Gimbels in particular). In 1982, Woodward & Lothrop had been purchased by Alfred Taubman, a mall developer, to thwart a hostile takeover attempt by Ron Baron. All this resulted in a multitude of conjecture with regard to the future of John Wanamaker, one of the oldest department stores in America.

Hilda was very happy being the couture buyer. Her trips to Paris and buying all these fine clothes really excited her. More speculation arose when Phil Hawley's right-hand man, Arden Batchelder, showed up at Wanamaker's. He had a reputation of being the hatchet man.

Batch, as he was called, was a crusty old merchant who had been president of the Emporium in San Francisco. His modus operandi was to dig into the data, ask a lot of questions, and then share his point of view. I felt like I did learn some things from him, and strangely, we seemed to get along well. Unbeknownst to me, he was observing my approach and calibrating my promotability. CHH believed in grooming its executives and twice sent me to take classes to focus on improving my management skills. I used to joke about it and tell people they were sending me to charm school.

My great friend from the Villa Cora
Antonio Burcini

Chris & Hilda at the Vatican
in Rome

Hilda on the Tiburon

Mad Cap with the Perez's

Man your battle stations

ARIZONA

In the early spring of 1986, I was summoned to Dick Boje's office under a cloak of secrecy. I had no idea what to expect. I was just told to come to his office immediately. Dick didn't mince any words. It was a Wednesday morning just before lunch. He told me to make plans to be in Phil Hawley's office on Thursday morning and to confirm my plans with Mr. Hawley's secretary. My heart was pounding when I realized that I had made arrangements to meet Joe in York, at the train show, as he was buying my 280ZX for his son Mike, and I couldn't go to LA until Sunday. I called Phil's secretary and made the arrangements to meet with Waldo Burnside (president of CHH) and then with Mr. Hawley, who would be at an AT&T board meeting Monday morning.

Unfortunately, this gave me several days to ponder my fate. Of course, I realized I wasn't being sent across the country to meet with the CEO of the company to get bad news; but given all the rumors surrounding JW, I was sure I was going to be transferred to the Emporium or the Broadway perhaps as executive vice president (EVP) of merchandising and marketing. I had never suspected what was actually going to happen regarding my career.

I arrived at the CHH offices in Downtown LA just before 8:00 a.m. (PST). Waldo immediately greeted me, and we headed to his office. Waldo was a fabulous executive, engaging, upbeat, and provocative. He was easy to talk with. What I liked most about him was his supportive style. As a point of interest, he had been the former president of Woodward and Lothrop. He certainly ranked high on my list of superb executives whom I had the privilege and pleasure to work with.

Waldo and I talked for about two hours about Wanamaker's, marketing, competitive positioning, and people. It was a totally uplifting conversation. At ten, we proceeded to Phil Hawley's office. I spent an hour with Phil. Most of the conversation centered on his vision for CHH. Phil also had an engaging style. At eleven, I met with Hart Lyon, executive vice president of CHH and a former CEO of the Broadway as was Phil.

Carter Hawley Hale Stores was formed by Ed Carter, owner of the Broadway in LA; Prentiss Hale, owner of the Emporium in San Francisco; and Phil Hawley, the star merchant of the Broadway and a superb executive. They had built a market-dominant group of stores primarily through merger and acquisition, only to be thwarted twice by hostile takeover attempts by the Limited stores. Part of the CHH strategy during this period was to merge the northern California stores into the Emporium, sell Wanamaker's (as had been widely rumored), and spin off the non-California stores of the Broadway for expansion into the southwest as a separate operating division. Most of this had been implemented already. I just couldn't pinpoint how I fit into all this, but I was soon to find out.

After forty-five minutes with Hart, Waldo and Phil entered the office and asked me to step outside for a few minutes. When they finished, they invited me to lunch with them in the CHH executive dining room. At this point, I still had no idea what was coming but did realize that the entire executive staff of CHH would see me, and that would certainly fuel speculation.

We were seated just before noon and immediately ordered. Then Phil took charge. "Bob, we've been very impressed with your performance at John Wanamaker over the past several years, and we all agree you are poised to take on a larger role. We'd like you to accept the position of president and chief executive officer of the Broadway Southwest (BSW)." He offered me a salary beyond my wildest expectations. "You will be eligible for bonuses and stock options commensurate with the position of CEO."

I was totally speechless. "What do you say?" I had never contemplated that I might jump over several other EVPs in the organization to be named CEO. I was so ecstatic that I could have flown back to Philadelphia without boarding the airplane. As is sometimes the case, there was one small problem. They wanted me to accept the position before they released the current CEO of the Broadway Southwest, Steve Marra. I had tons of questions but couldn't think clearly enough to ask more than a few. Furthermore, I had to sit on this news for over a month as a lame-duck senior VP at Wanamaker's. Phil arranged for his car and driver to take me to the Burbank Airport and bought me a first-class ticket for my return to Philadelphia.

As soon as I arrived at the airport, I went to a pay phone to call Hilda and share this spectacular news. She was excited for me but realized that if we were going to stay together, she'd have to give up her position at JW. Furthermore, she did not want to give up her trip to Paris for the November shows. Life does have a way of throwing those little curveballs at you every now and then.

First thing on Tuesday morning, I was in Dick's office at JW. Dick knew the headlines regarding me but was very curious about what other information Phil and Waldo might have shared. I confirmed that I knew Wanamaker's was being put up for sale and that I had been directed to keep all this quiet until CHH was ready to make a comprehensive announcement. The ensuing several weeks was tough for me. I was a classic lame duck but continued to behave as if I would be at JW for the rest of my career.

Shortly before my formal announcement, Jinx found out that I'd be moving to Arizona with Chris. She was devastated. For the first time since our very ugly divorce, I truly felt sorry for her. The announcement was made around the first of May in the Princeton Room at John Wanamaker. Some of my peers were congratulatory, especially Frank Tworecke, the GMM of men's and children's. Others were not pleased at all. I had ongoing disagreements with Kai Frost regarding our marketing, as well as Lloyd Haffner, our director of stores. Years later, they would find themselves even unhappier when I became their boss. Not long after my departure, Wanamaker's would be sold to Al Taubman and merged with Woodward & Lothrop.

On Mother's Day 1986, I boarded a flight to Phoenix to begin my tenure as CEO of the Broadway Southwest. It had been apparent to me that one of my most ardent supporters had turned out to be Arden Batchelder, who had agreed to work with me in transition for my first three months at BSW. He was a great sounding board.

Shortly after my appointment, I was again invited to another educational experience conducted by a couple of Yale professors. I always found these sessions to be extremely stimulating. At this particular one, we had dinner with John Wooden, the great UCLA basketball coach. His coaching philosophy was amazing. He focused on teamwork, not on the Xs and Os of plays. He set a standard of mutual respect among the players on his teams, winning ten national championships in his last twelve years of coaching.

Soon after my arrival, I realized that I had a number of problems to address, and I had a lot to learn about how to be an effective and successful CEO. Broadway Southwest hadn't become profitable as a stand-alone company. The work ethic was poor. We had some weak merchants and other executives. We had some older stores in need of updating. And we had made the decision to expand into Denver with some questionable locations. All these issues were most challenging, especially for a rookie CEO. However, I had plenty of time on my hands as I commuted from Philadelphia for three months.

During that time, I found a house in Paradise Valley that I was very excited about. I purchased it, somewhat to Hilda's dismay, and Chris and I (with all of Hilda's belongings) moved in during the one-hundred-plus-degree dog days of August so Chris could begin at Phoenix Country Day School. Hilda would continue to commute until she made her Paris market trip. We'd all be reunited and settled in for the holidays.

That Christmas, I gave Hilda an engagement ring. We were planning to get married sometime that spring. Hilda got serious about her tennis game, and I had joined the Boulders Golf Club in Carefree. I had made some significant management changes at BSW, replacing the apparel GMM with Patricia Van Cleave, who had been a superstar at May Company and at JW. She dived in and immediately began to grow the business.

That spring, in the hopes of getting pregnant, Hilda began to see a fertility specialist as she previously had two ectopic pregnancies and was told she would need to do in vitro fertilization. During this period, I expected Hilda's divorce to be finalized so that we might get married in June, but there were some delays. In July, we found out that Hilda was naturally pregnant. She sobbed like a baby; she was so ecstatic.

We finally got married in Sedona, Arizona, on August 29, 1987, with Chris as the best man and our friends Greg and John as our witnesses. In September of that year, Hilda and I honeymooned in Italy, staying first at the Villa d'Este on Lake Como, then the Villa Cora in Florence, and finally at the San Pietro in Positano. We had a truly sensational time.

That summer, I was being heavily recruited by the Bon Marché in Seattle. I really struggled with the prospect of leaving BSW and CHH as I felt an extreme loyalty to Phil, Waldo, and Batch for supporting my career development and to the team I'd built at BSW. Additionally, Hilda was pregnant, and I had a blossoming teenage son who loved Arizona. On the other hand, I was concerned that CHH wouldn't be able to support my long-term plans for expansion as we'd begun to retreat from the Denver market as a result of the changing competitive environment. However, the Bon Marché was making significant overtures.

Robert Campeau (an impulsive, risk-driven real estate developer from Canada) had taken over Allied Stores, the owner of such venerable names as Jordan Marsh, Maas Brothers, Stern's, Ann Taylor, Brooks Brothers, and the Bon Marché. He desperately wanted to hire some vibrant young management and made me an offer. Hilda and I discussed it at length. I informed Phil Hawley of the offer. Hawley countered, and I accepted. The Bon Marché wouldn't give up and made me an offer I couldn't refuse (guaranteed three years and a huge increase in salary). It was one of the toughest decisions of my career.

August 29, 1987

Shopping in Florence

Lunch

Capri

Cliff Diving in Position

Villa D' Este

10324 N. 49th Place

Grand Canyon 1986

1987 Tuxedo Man

Presentation to Arizona Republic

Lake Powell 1987

Chris & Hilda skiing in Purgatory

THE EMERALD CITY

Once again, I would move to temporary quarters before the full family move. At first, I was most certainly skeptical. Seattle seemed so far away from every place I was familiar with on the East Coast, and I knew very little about the Bon Marché. On the other hand, the compensation was very good, and my employment agreement provided for financial support in the event things didn't work out so well. Additionally, Hilda was excited about living in Seattle.

The first few months were crazy. First were all the management changes, primarily bringing Bob Morosky—the former head of operations at the Limited—on as president. Then in short order, there was the hostile takeover attempt by Campeau of my former employer, Federated Department Stores. On the other hand, the Bon Marché had numerous opportunities for improved performance. The merchandising was generally lackluster, with little focus on actually forecasting inventory management on sales as opposed to just filling the space. The merchant group was generally risk averse, so the concept of hitting hard on hot items by editing the assortments and owning products in depth wasn't the focus of the merchant group, and there were incongruities with regard to pricing categories. The company was efficient on logistics, finance, and systems; but like the Broadway, there was an embedded culture at the Bon that was difficult to overcome.

I quickly developed a program for my vision of the changes that needed to be implemented. I called it "power merchandising," my concept of intensifying key categories of merchandise. One of the executives (John Dahl) even wrote and performed a song for the management named "I Wanna Be a Power Merchant."

My favorite person to work with was the VP of marketing, John Buller, a very talented executive with exceptional leadership skills. John had played basketball at the University of Washington (in the then Pac-10). Their main rival was UCLA, where John Wooden had coached, and Buller had to defend against a player named Lew Alcindor. Alcindor, after turning pro, changed his name to Kareem Abdul-Jabbar and became the greatest scorer in the history of the NBA.

Bob Leigh was our senior VP of stores, a very professional and competent manager with quite the dry sense of humor. He did an outstanding job of implementing the merchandising plan through his visual manager, Ron Spencer, who made us all look good. Bob was also an outstanding expense manager. Finance and operations were under our EVP, Tom Harville, another great executive who would later actually become the CEO of the Bon.

My biggest challenge was the senior merchant team, most notably in women's apparel and accessories (my strongest suit). By and large, they were prisoners of their own experience and struggled with change. I did, over time, make several changes in the merchandising ranks, once again recruiting Patricia Van Cleave to come to the Bon and successfully recruiting a couple of former Macy's executives, Mike Balmuth (who would eventually become CEO of Ross Stores) and Bob Homler, former GMM of Macy's Home Store. This group of merchants did a superb job of implementing the "power merchant" concept.

During the recruiting process, I had been promised by Bob Campeau that Wilbur (Bill) Fix—the CEO—would be retiring within six months and that the EVP/CFO would take over his responsibilities, and I would add the title of CEO to being president. As it turned out, Fix just didn't want to retire. He had it made. He had a habit of gathering information from the key executives and presenting it to the corporate management as his own. He fundamentally had a poor work ethic that resulted in an absentee management style, allowing me to take charge and make things happen (as long as I reported everything to him for him to pass it on). The business began to take off.

While all this was happening, the takeover of Federated was coming together; and to my delight, upon its culmination, John Burden (my former boss from Burdines) was named CEO of Federated. John was always very supportive. The stars were truly aligned.

When the Federated merger was complete, I was given an additional perk— financial counseling or, as it would now be known, wealth management. After my divorce, I was beyond broke; I was in debt to the tune of about $30,000, which I had borrowed to buy my townhouse in Downtown Philadelphia. By the time I got financial counseling, five years later, I had significantly improved my net worth and was debt-free. At my first meeting with my new financial counselor, Larry Stack, he asked me what I believed was my largest asset. I said, "I suppose it's my house."

He set me straight right off the bat, telling me, "Your biggest asset is you and your ability to earn money and create wealth." Thus began a long and incredible relationship with Larry Stack; his firm, Brownson, Rehmus, and Foxworth (BRF); and subsequently Bob Patterson, along with Liz Roob Ireland. Over the years, they collectively guided me in building a multi-million-dollar net worth while still living a fulfilling and joyful lifestyle. I have stayed in touch with Larry since his and my retirement, mostly through having the great, good fortune to be on his list of friends with whom he shared political commentary and military history essays.

Bob Patterson and I bonded as well through golf and other common bonds. Bob has become my trusted adviser and one of my closest friends. Liz married Barney Ireland, who also worked at BRF, and they spent a good portion of the year at their hunting lodge (Forshalee) just north of Tallahassee. We were also good friends.

The Bon Marché had forty-plus stores in six states, covering the entire Pacific Northwest. We operated in Washington, Oregon, Idaho, Montana, Utah, and Wyoming. One of the great perks was a company plane, a King Air A200. It was really terrific. I did lease it once to go skiing in Sun Valley and got to fly it from Twin Falls, Idaho, to Boeing Field in Seattle. A couple of times, we flew it into the crater at Mount Saint Helens, which had erupted a few years earlier. We could transport eleven people in it and cruise at 250 miles per hour. It was a great perk.

Campeau had a Gulfstream G2 that I got to fly on several times. Twice, Campeau decided to have off-site management meetings. The first one in Bermuda involved golf. Bob claimed to have a hole in one on a par 4, but others in his group claimed he palmed the ball into the hole, which he no doubt did. The second trip was to his hunting lodge in Canada. Imagine all the heads of the nine divisions of FDS, plus the corporate team, camping out at his lodge in the middle of nowhere. We had a fishing tournament. I caught eighty trout, all eight inches long. Campeau had overstocked the lake.

Much to my surprise, life in Seattle offered us a plethora of great experiences. Our home overlooked the Admiralty Inlet of the Puget Sound. We bought a sailboat there and used it often, sailing to the San Juan Islands and around Puget Sound. We had great neighbors, particularly the Goddards and the Greggs. We settled into the social scene readily, with Hilda being named to the Seattle Ballet Board and me being appointed to the Seattle Chamber of Commerce and Patrons of Northwest Civic, Cultural, and Charitable Organizations (PONCHO), the who's who of Seattle. Hilda made friends with everyone she met. She was exceptionally happy with the prospect of having a baby in the spring of 1988.

Our miracle child, Sarah Elizabeth Mang, entered the world on March 9, 1988, about three weeks early. Unfortunately, I was in New York when Hilda went into labor, so Chris went to the University of Washington Hospital with her. I arrived back in Seattle about twelve hours after her birth. Hilda was a very, very happy mommy. We were all so thrilled, another "pinch me" moment in our lives. Everything seemed to be going so well. Additionally, we were enjoying our newfound friendships with Carl and Renee Behnke, Jimmy and

Patty Barrier, John and Rita Getzelman, Ron and Mila Hart, and Ron and Bonnie Elgin. We all vacationed together at every turn. Such a memorable group of friends.

When Lauren was about nine, she was spending some vacation time with us in Seattle. As I had done previously with Chris, I took her to see a therapist. Not much to my surprise, the therapist recommended I seek residential custody of Lauren. I did, and after a short battle, Lauren came to live with us. All my children together in this beautiful family environment was just overwhelming. We were all very happy.

On the other hand, while business at the Bon was the best in Federated, FDS was unable to service the debt that the company had incurred during the takeover and filed for Chapter 11 bankruptcy protection. Much to my dismay, John Burden resigned. I had such a collegial relationship with John; I knew I would miss him. Allen Questrom—the former president of Rich's and Bullock's, vice chairman of FDS, and CEO of Neiman Marcus—was brought in to replace him. Allen knew most of us, and we had a relatively seamless transition, other than dealing with the bankruptcy. Business at the Bon Marché continued to thrive. In 1990, we became the most profitable division of Federated on a percent-to-sales basis. Unfortunately for me, Bill Fix was still hanging on.

My relationships in the market continued to thrive. One of our major men's suppliers—Intercontinental Branded Apparel (IBA), a division of Hart Schaffner & Marx—staged several outings at Pebble Beach. Of course, a significant part of the agenda was golf, but IBA also had the license for Wimbledon. They brought in great pros to put on exhibitions and play with us amateurs. Hilda loved the events and played with the great Rod Laver one year. We also met a new friend there, John Lamb.

John was then, and still is, a "wild and crazy guy." John's wife at the time, Sue, was in the textile industry in Great Britain and a key supplier to IBA. Hence, they were also invited. We had an instant bonding, playing golf together at Pebble Beach, Cypress Point, and Spyglass Hill and tennis with Rod Laver, Ken Rosewall, and Roy Emerson. John and I became great friends.

In 1990, the first Goodwill Games was staged in Seattle. John Buller thought we should seize the opportunity to showcase our newly remodeled Downtown Seattle store with an event. For me, it was "déjà vu all over again." Calling on every connection we had, we assembled the most amazing gala and got it televised. Steve Largent of the Seattle Seahawks was the emcee, and we had performances throughout the night from Russian Cossack dancers, Diane Schuur, Bo Diddley, Otis Day and the Knights (of *Animal House* fame), and Dionne Warwick. We were stealing the retail platform from our two main competitors, Nordstrom and Frederick & Nelson.

With all the great things that were happening in my life, I had some concerns that Federated—under Allen's leadership—was beginning to consolidate major areas of responsibility under the corporate umbrella. Credit had been consolidated, and other "back-of-the-house functions" were on the threshold of being consolidated as well.

Early in 1991, Arnold Aronson had approached me through Levy Kerson to consider coming to Woodward & Lothrop (Woodies) and John Wanamaker. The prospect of returning (as the conquering hero) to JW was more than intriguing.

Wanamaker's—where I'd been a child model, where my mother had made her initial mark in retailing, where I had been senior vice president of the fashion store—was compelling. On the other hand, we loved living in Seattle, where we had great friends, where my future seemed bright, and where my family was very happy, so this added to the complexity. But Woodies/Wanamaker's wasn't just a division of a larger company; it was *the* company. The equity and compensation were significant, almost doubling my pay at the Bon Marché.

After laborious consideration, I decided to accept the offer. The linchpin was a five-year employment agreement personally guaranteed by Al Taubman, who had acquired JW after my departure. Over the years, I found the Taubmans to be of the highest integrity. Their word has been their bond, and they have lived up to every commitment they made to me. I respect them all immensely. Al was a legend. Bobby and Billy have carried the banner and continued to do the right things for their constituents and their employees. I am proud to have played a small role in their amazing history.

My resignation was not well received at Federated, and I quickly became persona non grata with Allen and Jim Zimmerman (then president of FDS). Time has a way of healing old wounds though. I have since rekindled my relationships with both Allen and Jim; oddly we are now all former employees of FDS. Jim owns a home in Hilton Head, and I have spent time with Allen recently at Arnold Aronson's sixtieth wedding anniversary party in New York City. We had a marvelous evening together.

16628 76th Ave West

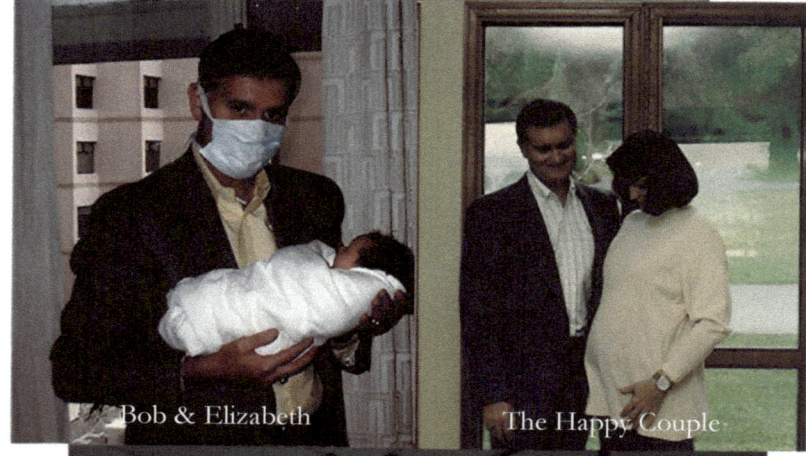

Bob & Elizabeth

The Happy Couple

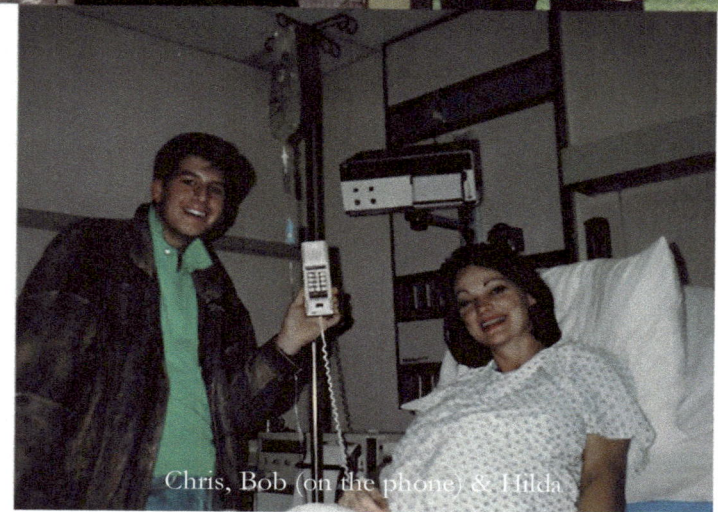

Chris, Bob (on the phone) & Hilda

Mt. Bachelor

Beaver Creek

Deer Valley

Seattle Friends in France

Seattle Friends Party

Family Portrait

Frank, Pat & Bob

Elizabeth in Seattle

The Paramour

John Burden & Bob winning
Division of the Year at Federated

Ninja Mang's

Bob & Frank

Bob Pat & Chris

Chris Senior Portraits

Mang kids

MY DREAM JOB

Relocating to Washington DC was very exciting for me, having been a self-proclaimed political junkie my entire adult life. DC is a modern-day Rome and the home of the most powerful government in the world. The city offers unparalleled cultural opportunities, including museums, theater, ballet, and opera.

One of my early acquaintances there was Larry Wilker, then president of the Kennedy Center, where Woodies had been one of the founding donors. Needless to say, we went there often. Twice, we attended the Kennedy Center Honors and rubbed shoulders with the likes of Gregory Hines, Jim Nabors, Carol Burnett, and even Audrey Hepburn, Hilda's all-time favorite. We actually sat in front of Mike Nichols and Diane Sawyer at one event and near the president's box in a subsequent one. The decision to relocate coincided with Chris starting college at Arizona State University (his first choice).

DC was also a city of great restaurants, where on any given night you might be seated across from someone in the cabinet, a senator, a governor, an ambassador, or any other politico. We definitely took advantage of the restaurant scene.

Hilda wasn't as thrilled to move to DC as I was, but as usual, she made lots of new friends and was, as always, the life of the party. After searching the housing market, we decided to live in Potomac, Maryland, just outside the famous beltway and on the north shore of the Potomac River. My commute was only about fifteen miles, but the traffic was generally terrible, so it took about forty-five minutes. We registered Lauren at Potomac Elementary for the fifth grade. Ironically, Hilda ran into one of her college girlfriends, Mary Jane O'Dell, at a parent-teacher meeting at the school. They were both absolutely delighted to reunite. Hilda really immersed herself into life in Potomac, playing lots of tennis, lunching with the "housewives of Potomac" and being a dedicated mommy.

Working at Woodies and returning to Wanamaker's was both exciting and challenging for me. I was thrilled with the prospect of working with Arnold Aronson, who had an amazing résumé. After graduating from Harvard and Columbia Business School, Arnold went to Bloomingdale's. After a stint at May LA, Arnold was president of Bullock's and Saks Fifth Avenue and later CEO of BATUS Retail—the owners of Gimbels, Marshall Field's, Kohl's, and Frederick & Nelson in Seattle. The combined companies of Woodies and Wanamaker's had not performed well in about seven years, and Arnold and I were determined to turn that performance around.

Both the Philadelphia and Greater DC markets had seen a lot of new competition as the real estate developers moved to create megamalls by persuading Macy's, Bloomingdale's, Abraham & Straus, Lord & Taylor, and

Nordstrom to expand into these densely populated markets. Additionally, the May Company had invested heavily in Hecht's to compete with not only Woodies but also with all the other upscale new competition. Nevertheless, we felt that with intensified and more focused inventories, plus a more powerful multimedia marketing thrust, we would get the business headed in the right direction, and it did.

Our board was composed of Al Taubman, Bobby Taubman, Bernard Winograd, and Bob Larsen, as well as Arnold, myself, and Bob Mulligan, the longtime vice chairman of Woodies. I particularly enjoyed Larsen, who was on the government's Resolution Trust board that had been formed to oversee the refinancing of some government-backed investments. Larsen was extremely positive and very much the big-picture guy. I had great admiration for Al, really liked Bobby, and thought Bernard Winograd was one of the smartest people I'd ever met.

We had a phenomenal relationship with the *Washington Post*. I would meet with Donald Graham regularly and, on occasion, with his mother, Kay (of Watergate fame). On a few occasions, I dined with Ben Bradlee (also of Watergate fame). He was a real guy's guy. He had been very close to John Kennedy. Years later, I would meet my all-time favorite columnist, Art Buchwald, but not through the *Post*. It seemed Buchwald was a foster child who'd been taken in by the Markay family (Larry Diamond's in-laws) and had become friends with Larry Diamond. Larry seated us together at his fiftieth wedding anniversary party. It was an amazing evening. Lauren Mang was my date. What an evening for us both!

In his mid-sixties, my father developed a tremor. Shortly thereafter, he was diagnosed with Parkinson's disease, likely brought on by the head trauma he had suffered in WWII. Subsequently, he had a TIA (ministroke) while driving and hit another car. His driver's license was revoked on the spot. For the next few years, he spent most of his time sitting in his Niagara chair in front of the TV. After suffering two strokes, he passed away at the age of seventy-one on December 24, 1992, at Sarasota Memorial Hospital with my brother, Frank, at his bedside. Ironically, it was Hilda's forty-third birthday. Losing my father was heartbreaking, but observing his decline with Parkinson's was even worse. Seeing this WWII hero's demise seemed so unfair.

In the spring of 1993, the Taubmans decided to take their real estate company public and informed us at a board meeting they would need to sell Woodies and Wanamaker's to avoid any conflict of interest. Arnold had negotiated a right of first offer in his employment agreement, so we were given a limited amount of time to put together an offer.

Coinciding with this, early one evening in 1993, Hilda called her dear friend Mary Jane while I was at work and complained of abdominal pains. Unbeknownst to me, they went to the emergency room at Georgetown Medical Center. Mary Jane called me at home sometime after eight and told me I needed to come there ASAP. Hilda was in writhing pain, and her doctor recommended an emergency hysterectomy. He said she had an ovarian cyst. She had great faith in her doctor, and seeing her in all this pain, we really had no choice. Postoperative tests were performed, and we were told there wouldn't be any need for follow-up. Boy, were they ever wrong!

Arnold and I spent much of our time in the fall of 1993 meeting with potential investors in an attempt to finance a purchase of the company. The company had incurred a lot of debt over the years, and it had become increasingly hard to pay its high interest. We needed to structure an offer that would be acceptable to the Taubmans. Unfortunately, any offer would involve some significant write-offs by all the investors. A meeting was planned for January, after we would have the Christmas business results, to be in a position to better understand all the implications involved in this potential sale. The meeting was scheduled for January 14, 1994 (Arnold's birthday), at the Taubman offices in New York, right across the street from Trump Tower.

11000 Riverwood Drive

Lynn Swann & Bob

Larry Diamond, Bob & Art Buchwald

Ice Skating at The Greenbrier

Bob, Elizabeth & Hilda

Harley Bob

Hilda at Christmas

THE TIMES, THEY ARE A-CHANGING

As we assembled to meet, I was overwhelmed by the number of true power brokers in the room—Ace Greenberg, CEO of Bear Stearns at the time; Tony James, who would later become the billionaire head of Blackstone; and of course the Taubman team. The meeting didn't really last that long. The bid was rejected as a result of the gap in financing.

After the meeting, Al Taubman asked me to step into his office. Arnold, feeling the pain of rejection from a decent offer for a debt-ridden company, left with his/our advisers. Al said to me, "Arnold is going to resign from the company as a result of this decision. We hope that you will take over as CEO. Given your experience at Federated, I'm confident that you'll be able to manage us through a Chapter 11 filing as we try to sell this company under the protection of the courts. I will personally guarantee your income, employment agreement, and long service to both Woodies and Wanamaker's. I trust this will be acceptable to you?" It was an offer you can't refuse.

On January 17, 1994 (Martin Luther King Day), the front page of the *Washington Post* was dedicated to a massive earthquake in Northridge, California. However, the front page of the business section was dedicated to Woodward & Lothrop filing for protection to reorganize under the bankruptcy code (Chapter 11). It was the buzz of Washington.

I learned when I was at the Bon Marché that few people understood the bankruptcy code. Chapter 11 allowed you to reorganize the financial structure of the company with the agreement of a committee of creditors. Generally, it did relate to performance; but as was the case in the Federated filing, the primary reason for this filing was the mountain of debt. Chapter 11 was a management tool to clean up the balance sheet and, in this case, sell the company.

We formed a creditor committee that included representatives of the bankers, the vendors (who had a vested interest in a successful outcome), the union, and the retired executives. Representing the secured lenders was Wilbur Ross, the current secretary of commerce in the Trump administration. Jones Day (law firm) represented the creditors, and Wilkie Farr & Gallagher represented us. Our attorneys, Myron Trepper and Marc Abrams, were superb. Our investment banker, the Argosy Group, also did a great job.

The department store business was complicated enough, but adding the job of managing the bankruptcy made it extremely complex. I had a terrific administrative assistant, Barbara Dempsey, and a great staff assistant, David Faircloth, as well as a competent team of merchants. Despite the filing, the business continued to perform reasonably well. We had very little disruption in inventory flow as we were able to readily obtain debtor-in-possession financing.

In February 1994, I hired my niece Kristen Coradini as an assistant buyer in the lingerie area. She had recently graduated from the University of South Carolina with a degree in business. When she came on board, a number of people thought she'd been hired as a model because she was so statuesque. Kristen did a great job and was very well liked. Later, she would be hired by Macy's in the Tysons Corner store.

Incredibly, in the midst of all this going on, on May 11, 1994, I was honored by the fashion accessories industry at the annual charity ball, the Fashion Accessories Benefit Ball (FABB). It was a truly wonderful evening. I was exceptionally proud as was my mother, who was able to attend. Dick Fields presented me, and my guests of honor were Hilda (of course), Elizabeth, Larry and Janet Diamond, Boris Kliot (the owner of Riviera), Bob Melzer, and my great friend Bert Perez. In attendance were about two thousand guests from the industry. When I took Elizabeth (then six years of age) to the podium with me, after the oohs and aahs, you could've heard a pin drop, very unusual in a banquet of that magnitude. I gave a short "thank you" speech.

Much of my time in 1994 was spent in reorganization meetings in New York, Washington, and Detroit. Flying in Al Taubman's G5 was a special treat. A private aircraft is the ultimate perk.

The department store industry was in a downward spiral largely due to the debt accumulated during the leveraged takeovers of the '80s. The Broadway and Macy's were also in bankruptcy. Federated had successfully emerged under Allen Questrom's leadership and was now looking for acquisitions to strengthen their market share. As developers continued to expand their malls, cross-channel shopping became more prevalent, and stores like Kohl's and

Target were gaining share. Walmart was now the largest retailer in the country, while Sears and J. C. Penney limped along.

One of the really fun events opening up 1995 and held in the downtown Woodies store was sponsored by the art society honoring Tony Curtis. (He was being celebrated in Washington DC for his contributions to the arts.) I flew my mother up for the event. Tony came in early with his girlfriend (Jill) directly from Paris, where he had been honored by the French film industry. We spent some time together before the evening's festivities. When we met, it was like talking to a friend; but after my introduction and he went onstage, he became the amazing actor he was. He was really engaging and put on quite a performance. My favorite movie had always been *Some Like It Hot*, in which he starred with Jack Lemmon and Marilyn Monroe, so this made it even more special for me.

Early in 1995 at the Millrose Games (a track meet held at Madison Square Garden and originally founded by John Wanamaker as a track meet between his NY store and his Philadelphia store), I was able to present the winner of the Wanamaker Mile, Graham Hood, the trophy. I had been on the Millrose board in the '80s but never had the privilege of presenting the trophy before.

Reorganizing Woodies and Wanamaker's was a daunting task. The going concern value of the company would have resulted in the creditors taking a huge write-down. On the other hand, our competitors didn't want to lose market share if the company was sold to one or the other. And the book value of the assets was worth much more than the going concern value. I spent some time meeting with Jim Zimmerman in an attempt to make a deal with Federated to buy the company. When they offered us $550 million for the assets, we announced an agreement to sell. Thus began a bidding war between Federated and the May Company. After an in-court auction in August of 1995, we successfully sold the assets of the company to May Department Stores and J. C. Penney. After liquidating the inventory, the transaction amounted to $970 million, arguably the most successful bankruptcy sale in the annals of retailing. The Taubmans were extremely pleased with the outcome and treated me well.

Hilda and I had decided to go to Africa that September with a group of our Seattle friends. We had a spectacular trip going to Johannesburg; the Kruger National Forest; Zimbabwe, where we canoed the upper Zambezi River and white-water-rafted the lower part of the river below Victoria Falls; Botswana; and the Okavango Delta, ending our adventure in Cape Town. Upon our return that September, Hilda threw me a surprise fiftieth birthday party. She had invited all my closest friends, as well as our Washington friends. It was a spectacular evening. Little did we know that our lives would take a huge turn for the worst in October.

Bob introducing Tony Curtis

Jill, Tony Curtis & Pat

Beaux Arts Ball

FABB Presentation

The FABB Table

Sue Nodine, Bob & Joyce Mantyla

Dick Fields, Bob & Joyce Mantyla

Dee Perez & Bob with Bert Perez & others

The Birthday Boy

Sue Nodine speech to Bob at his 50th Birthday

THE BATTLE OF A LIFETIME

In October of 1995 while I was attending a board meeting at Shady Grove Hospital, I was called out of the meeting to take an emergency phone call. (Hilda was meeting with her doctor in DC.) When I got on the phone with the doctor, he suggested I come to his office immediately. When I arrived, he told me that Hilda had a grapefruit-size tumor in her abdomen and several other smaller tumors. He recommended we go immediately to Georgetown Medical Center and schedule emergency surgery. That afternoon, the head of surgery at Georgetown Medical Center performed about a four-hour surgical procedure on Hilda, removing the large tumor, three golf-ball-size tumors, and multiple pearl-size tumors.

Hilda's friends Chris Assad, Diane Magruder (Bruce), Ann Seymour, and Sally Schowalter all came to the hospital to sit with me and wait to hear the results of her surgery. When the surgeon came down to deliver the news, he was direct, suggesting I immediately contact an oncologist. My knees buckled, and I nearly collapsed. It was now painfully obvious that the diagnosis and prognosis before her hysterectomy in 1993 were incorrect. She had lived with untreated cancer for two years without symptoms.

After I left the hospital at around ten thirty that night, the doctor paid a visit to Hilda and gave her the news. His bedside manner was questionable, but delivering the news at that hour of the night when nobody was there to comfort her was inconsiderate and reckless in my opinion. After he left the room, Hilda ripped out her IVs and attempted to leave the hospital. Clearly, she was delusional. Fortunately, she didn't get too far. Hilda had a miraculous ability to recover and was only hospitalized for a few days.

Foremost in our lives now, we had two major decisions to make—the choice of an oncologist and a medical protocol. My friend Dr. Henry Wise (a urologist) recommended the oncologist. The decision on medical protocol was difficult. The gynecological cancer group recommended bleomycin, etoposide, and cisplatin. Hilda met with the people at Emory, and we both discussed treatment options with Deborah Armstrong, head of the GYG at Johns Hopkins. The alternative protocol was a combination of Taxol (interestingly a drug discovered in the Chemistry Department at FSU) and carboplatin.

Hilda's tumors were not the garden variety, known as epithelial cell tumors. Hers were quite rare, only seven documented cases at the time. They were some form of germ cell tumors that were slower growing and necrotic in nature (more stubborn and resistant to treatment). We opted for the Taxol/carboplatin protocol as it seemed to be the more aggressive path. Radiation was a third option, but we felt that it would limit future surgical options.

While all this was going on, I was interviewing for positions to continue my career. My best two options were with Sears in Chicago and Duty Free Shoppers

(DFS) in San Francisco. Medical treatment and cancer research was highly rated at Stanford, but the Duty Free job would require extensive worldwide travel. It was quite the juggling act, but our priority was the medical care. It actually turned out to be the better alternative.

The transition to the Bay Area took us several months. While Hilda continued her chemo treatments in DC, I began my stint as vice chairman of DFS in January of 1996. Hilda had thus far tolerated the chemo well. However, before our move, she was rushed to the hospital, and the oncologist located me in Sydney, Australia. I immediately flew to San Francisco and then onto DC to be at her bedside. Chemo treatments are highly toxic, and after multiple rounds, the side effects can be painful and risky. Such was the case in this instance as Hilda had developed a fistula that needed repair. After her recovery, we discontinued the chemo as her tests had suggested she was cancer-free.

In July of 1996, we had settled in Atherton, only three miles from Stanford and one of the most upscale areas in the South Bay. We both fell in love with the house and the neighborhood. We established a relationship with the Stanford Medical Center immediately—first with Dr. Brandon Sikic, a highly respected cancer researcher, and then with Dr. Nelson Teng, an exceptional gynecological surgeon. Additionally, a friend of mine from my days at CHH (David Folkman) introduced me via telephone to his brother Dr. Judah Folkman, a world-renowned cancer research doctor at Dana-Farber Institute in Cambridge, Massachusetts.

Unfortunately, the DFS job was not what I expected. After a year, we parted company on the heels of DFS being sold to LVMH, the famous French luxury brand house. I took several months off as Hilda's cancer had returned, and she had started on an experimental treatment.

In 1997, I accepted a position in New York City to be the CEO of Monet Inc., a highly recognized manufacturer and supplier of fashion jewelry. We agreed that I would commute between New York and San Francisco, once again creating complicated logistics for our family. Chris had now graduated from James Madison University and accepted a position with Macy's in San Francisco.

Lauren, through Hilda's insistent efforts, was attending Sacred Heart High School. Elizabeth was in public school for the third grade but would move to Saint Joseph's Elementary, the feeder school to Sacred Heart. I would typically fly to NY on the Sunday night red-eye and return to San Francisco Thursday afternoon, arriving in time for dinner and a long weekend. One week each month, I would spend the week in California. I did get quite a bit of quality time at home with family. The first year, Hilda underwent another surgery to debulk her tumors, followed by new chemo treatments.

Judah Folkman collaborated with Nelson Teng and Brandon Sikic, and they decided to put Hilda on thalidomide, a drug that had been taken off the market. It had been used as a sleep aid for pregnant women in the sixties but resulted in deformities of the fetus. Nevertheless, it was determined that the drug retarded the growth of rapidly growing cells, like tumors. Hilda had some problems tolerating the drug as it made her tired and sleepy.

It became of paramount importance to both of us that we regularly scheduled high-quality time together. We traveled together to Hong Kong, Singapore, Bali, and Hawaii during my time at DFS and subsequently planned regular trips to Hawaii. Hilda loved Hawaii, and we managed to cover every island. Ultimately, we landed regularly on Maui and joined the Grand Wailea Club. We spent a number of family holidays there, often with the Himots.

Leslie Himot had been Hilda's dearest friend since they were in their early teens, growing up on Selfridge Air Force Base, just outside Detroit. They were inseparable. I had gotten to know Ed and Leslie when Hilda and I were living together in Philadelphia. Over the ensuing years, we spent a lot of time together. They adopted two boys, David and Wesley.

We often spent the holidays with them, once skiing in Colorado and multiple times in Hawaii and Hilton Head, where they built their "beach house." Leslie agreed to be Elizabeth's godmother when she was born. Accepting this was of exceptional importance to Hilda.

In June of 1998, Hilda and I took Chris, Sabelle, Lauren, and Elizabeth to Italy for a family vacation. We flew into Rome and did all the sights there before heading to Florence. We stopped in Orvieto on the way; checked into the Villa Cora, my all-time favorite hotel; and began our gastronomic tour of Tuscany. We were actually in San Gimignano when they were filming *Tea with Mussolini*. Afterward, Chris and Sabelle went to Positano, and the girls and I went to Paris and stayed with Josie Natori.

Hilda had suffered through several surgeries from 1997 to 2000, debulking her tumors and resecting her liver. I was able to be with her through each of these. Her ability to recover was truly miraculous, but each subsequent surgery would take its toll.

In June of 1999, Lauren would graduate from Sacred Heart with honors and go on to attend Villanova University in September. We were all so very proud of Lauren's accomplishments. She made great grades, played softball, and developed an amazing cadre of friends. Lauren has always been the glue in keeping her friends together throughout her life.

For the millennium, we planned a great week of celebration at the Grand Wailea in Maui that would include Hilda's fiftieth birthday party. Hilda's dearest friends from Michigan Ed and Tina Marcuz, Leslie and Ed Himot, Rita and John Getzelman, the Zars, Jeff and Marcia Rohr, Jimmy and Patty Barrier, Carl and Renee Behnke, and Jim and Ga Hanna all came. We partied almost every night, spent a day sailing on the *Trilogy*, played golf, went to a luau, and rang in the year 2000 with great vigor. It was a most memorable event.

During all this, I was commuting to NY, working to build Monet at a difficult time in the department store business. Stores were demanding gross margin support from suppliers while cutting their space allocations at point of sale to launch the onslaught of new designer licenses. On top of that, retail consolidation had left Monet with a small handful of customers. We were highly reliant on Federated (FDS) and May Company, giving them enormous leverage. To more effectively compete, I initiated a plan to reduce our reliance on domestic manufacturing to improve margins and more readily support the retailers. Additionally, expanding our channels of distribution was not well received by FDS and May.

While I had significantly improved the performance and cash flow at Monet, it was a futile battle. Compounded by the commute, I felt it was time to move on. I left in January of 2000. Shortly after my departure, the company was sold to Liz Claiborne. Once again, I would take a sabbatical and spend time with family in Atherton.

On July 7, 2000, Kristen married her longtime boyfriend, David Lentine, in Bluemont, Virginia. It was a beautiful wedding venue, and the event itself was wonderful. Hilda's mother, brother, and sister, Edie, were there, and everyone had a marvelous time. David had become a very successful entrepreneur in the valet business and was thrilled to make Kristen his wife.

On July 29, 2000, Chris married his longtime love, Sabelle, in a garden ceremony and reception at our home in Atherton. There were about one hundred guests. I had the great privilege to serve as Chris's best man. Hilda did an amazing job of planning, organizing, and staging the wedding. We had a wedding dinner party that also included family, as well as a morning-after brunch for all the people who had come from afar to attend the wedding. It made for one of the most memorable events of our lives.

Chris and Sabelle had met at James Madison University, where he finished his bachelor's degree after transferring from Arizona State. Sabelle referred to Chris as "history guy" since she first met him in a history class. Sabelle is younger than Chris, so he graduated before her. Amazingly, they were able to keep a long-distance relationship until her early graduation, when they would share a great apartment on the back side of Nob Hill in San Francisco. Chris was working at Macy's, and Sabelle had taken a job with an investment bank. Chris proposed on Sabelle's birthday, October 14, 1999, on his knee at Julius' Castle Restaurant to cheers from the other diners when she accepted. As they say, "The rest is history."

After the wedding, Hilda and I took Elizabeth with us on our second trip to Africa. We went again with some of our Seattle friends to Londolozi, Ngorongoro Crater in Tanzania, the Serengeti, and the private island of Memba off the coast of Tanzania, where Elizabeth got scuba certified at the age of twelve in the Indian Ocean. All in all, it was another amazing adventure in our lives.

425 Walsh Road

Kristen & David
Lentine

Elizabeth & Josie Natori in Paris

Father Daughter Dance

Mang's & Himot's Maui

Sabelle & Hilda

Mang Family Maui 2000

Chris & Sabelle's Wedding

Bob & Elizabeth fishing in Alaska

Elizabeth caught a
Salmon in Alaska

Father Daughter Dance

Bob at Monet

Sunset in Serengeti

Bob, Hilda & Elizabeth in the Seregenti

Dinner on the beach in Memba, Africa

HOOSIERS

After we returned from Africa, we were faced with another career decision. I had turned down an offer to move to Indianapolis twice primarily because we wanted to stay in California, even though the company was exciting, and the opportunity to expand the business was superb.

In October 2000, I accepted the position to become the CEO of Galyan's Trading Company, a large category-killer format in the sporting goods business. Galyan's was composed of fifteen stores located in Indiana, Minnesota, Ohio, Chicago, and Greater Washington DC. The Limited had acquired the company from Pat Galyan, the founder's son, and decided to sell a significant interest in it to a Los Angeles private equity firm, Freeman Spogli. I had met them through Norman Matthews, who had been on the Monet board and had been the former president of Federated back when Howard Goldfedder was the CEO and when John Burden and Allen Questrom were vice chairmen. The plans were to rapidly expand the company's presence in existing markets and into new markets and take the company public. While neither Hilda nor I were very excited about moving to Indiana, I was superexcited with the prospect of building the Galyan's business and taking the company public.

By October 2000, Hilda had been through five surgeries and multiple chemo treatments and was facing one more surgery. The sixth would be her final surgical procedure; as she had so much scar tissue, she wouldn't be able to tolerate another one. We connected with an oncologist in Indiana who had been at MD Anderson, and Hilda began radiation treatments. Between the outstanding work of Nelson Teng and the brilliant medical advice from Judah Folkman, in addition to Hilda's amazing recuperative ability, Hilda was able to live a generally good quality of life, long beyond the early predictions of her demise. We continued to travel abroad numerous times and enjoy life as much as possible.

In June of 2001, I took Galyan's public while Hilda and Elizabeth enjoyed the south of France together. I caught up with them in Italy, and we spent two more weeks enjoying our time with one another. The IPO was a huge success, being oversubscribed sixfold. Opening and closing the Nasdaq was really great.

My time at Galyan's, for the most part, was very exciting. In the sporting goods business, you got to attend some great events. Chris and I were able to attend the Salt Lake City Winter Olympics in 2002. We saw the hockey team play and lots of ski events (actually on skis) on the slopes. I also was able to attend the Cast and Blast hunting and fishing event at the Little Bighorn in Montana. My old friend from Wanamaker's Frank Tworecke was also there, and we went fly-fishing together. It was a *blast*.

Galyan's also sponsored the Pacers, where we had a skybox, and the Colts, where we had great seats, but we were often invited to sit in the owner's box.

One of our neighbors, Billy Brooks, had been a receiver in the NFL and worked for the Colts. It was great fun to toss the football around with him. We also liked his wife, Holly, very much. Another neighbor with whom our family became great friends were Lynn and Isiah Thomas. Isiah was coaching the Pacers at the time. We both really enjoyed getting to know them, and Elizabeth was friendly with their children, Josh and Lauren. We stayed connected with them when they moved to New York. We visited them at their home in Purchase over the Christmas holidays in 2005. Isiah and Lynn were great with Elizabeth, even allowing her to stay with them when she interned with the New York Knicks during her senior year at Hilton Head Prep.

Being in the sporting goods business was like being a kid in a candy store. Testing the equipment and relating to much of the product was stimulating. We had a fabulous relationship with Nike through our local Nike rep, Michael "Beck" Bechert. Beck and I became great friends and still see each other whenever we can, of course, always involving a game of golf. I was able to join Crooked Stick Golf Club, one of the top courses in the country and home to the famous golf course architect Pete Dye. Another of my thrills in golf was playing with Pete Dye and the legendary University of North Carolina basketball coach Dean Smith in a charity event.

I was able to build a great team of merchants at Galyan's, enticing my great friend Bob Wechsler to come to Indiana and run our sporting goods equipment business, Jeff Brown from May Company Pittsburgh to run our apparel business, and Ed Whitehead—who had previously been with Ralph Lauren, Calvin Klein, and Harrods in London—to lead our marketing efforts. I was fortunate to retain Chris's close friend Michael Greenberg to build our direct-to-consumer business as well as provide invaluable customer insights. He commuted from San Francisco; as it turned out, it was a very wise move on his part.

Bob Wechsler and I truly enjoyed renewing our friendship, both personally and professionally. We shared the same vision on how to grow a business and had great success together at Galyan's. My nephew David Coradini had received his MBA at Georgia Southern, having been captain of the basketball team, and we fast tracked him into a buyer's job in the sports equipment zone. Business was growing as were profits for the first three years. Things, once again, took a bad turn in 2004. Hilda's health was deteriorating more rapidly at the same time when the owners of Galyan's were most anxious to "cash out." That spring, we decided to make our final move together.

One of the last big thrills of my Galyan's years took place in Chicago, where we now had six stores. I was invited to throw out the first pitch at a Chicago Cubs game. I practiced for a week because I was afraid I'd throw a dirt ball, but when I got to the mound, I sailed the pitch right over the catcher's head.

1089 Laurelwood

Opening the NASDAQ

Galyan's IPO at the NASDAQ

David & Kelley
Coradini

Elizabeth Rock
Climbing

Senator Lugar & Bob

Bob & Billy Williams

Joe Houck, Bob & Robbie Gordon at Indy 500

HHI

In June of 2003, Lauren graduated from Villanova with a degree in art history and a 3.5 GPA. We were very proud of her. Jinx attended the ceremony, and it was the last time I saw her. Also during 2003, Hilda and I began to seriously consider our next move. Hilda did not want to move to Florida, where I had yearned to retire. (Paramount in her mind was that Elizabeth should be close to her dearest lifelong friend Leslie.) Ed and Leslie had a beach house in Hilton Head, where we had vacationed together often. (As her illness progressed, Hilda's need to be near Leslie increased dramatically.) We had half-heartedly looked for a few years and finally found a house we liked very close to Leslie and Ed. We closed the sale in August of 2003.

My departure from Galyan's began to unfold in February 2004. I agreed to stay with the company for ninety days while the board searched for my replacement. It was again tough enough to be a lame duck, but now with the additional complexity of Hilda's deteriorating health and our prospective move to Hilton Head, it was overwhelming. When school was out in June, we began our migration south. We connected with a local oncologist, who was not of much help, and registered Elizabeth at Hilton Head Prep as it was very important to Hilda that Elizabeth be educated in the south. It was also of greatest importance that she finish high school in Hilton Head and that I commit to being a full-time dad. That agreement all but sealed my retirement.

By this time, Hilda was pretty much bedridden as her disease had severely metastasized, and we were using hospice daily. Chris, Sabelle, and Lauren (who flew down on an emergency basis) joined us for Labor Day, at which point Hilda was only given a few days to live. On September 9, 2004, at 11:35 p.m., she passed away. We were all there with her during her final moments. The next few weeks were terrible. As she had requested, we had her remains cremated in Hilton Head and had her funeral service and interment in Knoxville. It was her wish to be next to her grandmother, and there she lay today.

For the next several weeks, I ran on adrenaline, getting Elizabeth settled into Hilton Head Prep and considering what I might be able to do professionally from Hilton Head. I managed to get a few consulting gigs and served on two boards, but that was extremely difficult to manage from a "barrier island." I did join Sea Pines Country Club and managed to get in some regular golf groups. I made a handful of great friends through golf there. Jim Hooper, Jim Risinger, Vinny Ahooja, Tommy Taylor, and Bubba Eldridge remained close friends today. Tommy had a house on the fourteenth hole at Harbour Town, where we partied all week long of the Heritage. Tommy and I played in two pro-ams together, finishing second in one.

Year 2005 was mostly uneventful for me. I worked with a few clients, did the best I could to be father and mother, and concentrated on being of some value to the boards I was on. Things didn't work out on the Sur La Table board as Freeman Spogli (the former owners of Galyan's) took control and, in my opinion, wanted to stack the board with members who were loyal to them. For some reason, I didn't fit the character. Christopher and Banks was a different story. I had serious concerns with the management plan, especially as it related to inventory control. After we parted company, the stock took a huge hit because, as I had predicted, the inventory backed up on them, resulting in a serious deterioration of margins and profits.

In September of 2005, my children threw a sixtieth birthday party for me in Las Vegas. We also dedicated a night to celebrating Hilda's life with gospel singers and lots of fun and frolic. We stayed at the Paris Hotel on the strip, gambled some, played golf, went to the show O, and generally had a great week. My dear friend Sue Nodine was there, as well as Dick and Kathy Fields, Michael and Delia Bechert, the Himots, Ken and Sue Goldman, Ned and Joanie Castleberry, and Dennis BeMent. Some of our Seattle friends came as well— Rita Getzelman, the Behnkes, Jim and Ga Hanna, Ron and Mila Hart, and Chris's and my friends the Greenbergs. We all partied heartily.

Ten years later, we would celebrate my seventieth birthday in California wine country at the home of our close friends Michael and Gloria Greenberg, near Healdsburg. It was a more intimate smaller get-together that included Chris; Sabelle; Chiara; Lauren and Elizabeth; Jim Zimmerman and his lovely wife, Ingrid; Caryn Beck-Dudley, who was now the dean of the Leavy School of Business at Santa Clara University; and Ann, who had become (and still is) the woman in my life. It was an amazing several days of touring and tasting, culminating with a most memorable evening at Kistler Winery, where we were treated to an unforgettable meal prepared by a three-star Michelin chef. I would say we may not have overindulged, but we certainly consumed an abundant sufficiency.

Denis Bement & Bob

Sabelle & Chris

Michael & Delia Bechert

Dick & Kathy Fields

60th Birthday in Vegas

Dick Fields, Lauren & Sabelle

Sue Nodine & Bob

Renee Benke & Bob

Larry 'Ace' Diamond & Bob

Pat & Bob Christmas

Chiara at the helm

Bob & Sue Nodine in France

Sue Nodine in France

Ann & Sabelle

Kistler Fanatic

Bob, Chiara & John Caldwell

70th Birthday Celebration

BACK TO FSU

In 2006, I was invited to join the Florida State University College of Business Board of Governors by Caryn Beck-Dudley, dean of the College of Business. My very close friend Jeff Rohr had been heavily involved with FSU's College of Business as well as the FSU Foundation and sponsored my nomination. I was deeply moved. This honor would be of major consequence to the rest of my life. I loved my time at FSU and felt strongly that my decision to attend FSU catapulted my career.

In August of 2006, Lauren moved to London to pursue her master's degree through Sotheby's Institute of Art after working for Christie's and the Howard Greenberg Art Gallery in NYC. I visited her a few times that year. Lauren wrote a blog about her time in England. It was a great tool for me to follow her.

In 2007, Elizabeth graduated from Hilton Head Prep and went on to attend the University of South Carolina. Her mother would have been thrilled. She wanted to follow in her mother's footsteps and major in psychology. Like most college kids, though, she majored in fun. Elizabeth certainly enjoyed her college years, befriending a number of football players who lived in the same building (as did Steve Spurrier, who needs no introduction). Life continued in limbo for a while—engaging in Elizabeth's college years, attending some football games, and scheduling family time together during the holidays. Chris was now living in New York as Macy's had consolidated operations, and he was fortunate enough to be selected to be a part of the corporate team.

Lauren would, as always, continue to excel academically and get her master's degree in 2007 (with distinction) after having an amazing experience living in London. She would return to New York City and work for Sotheby's for a period.

Certainly, the latter part of 2008 was financially devastating. Political decisions over time, including bankers taking bad paper to extend loans to less than creditworthy buyers, resulted in the biggest downturn in the markets since 1929. I lost more money than I ever thought I would earn when I was younger. At the same time, my ability to earn an income had dried up. My golf game wasn't improving either. And with Elizabeth now off at college, I was an empty nester, albeit with two beautiful golden retrievers, named Ricky and Lucy. One of the highlights of my days was walking the dogs. I also had the freedom to travel more often and continued to connect with John Lamb in Mallorca each summer. My involvement at FSU grew, and I had developed a great reputation as a board member.

On December 15, 2008, my darling mother would lose her battle with pulmonary heart disease. Joe, Pat, Frank, Barbara, and I were with her when she passed away. It was devastating for us all. The worst part for me was realizing I would never again get to talk to her, ask her questions, or tell her "I love you."

Even today, I often think of the sacrifices she made for me and what an inspiration she was in so many ways.

On September 9, 2009, five years to the day after Hilda's death, I got a phone call while playing golf with my son, Chris, and Ray Bragg—the head pro at Sea Pines Country Club—that would lift my spirits immensely. The call was from Caryn Beck-Dudley, dean of the College of Business, informing me of my nomination to FSU Business School Hall of Fame. Having worked during my college days, I wasn't really known as a BMOC or big man on campus. Hall of Fame recognition from my university meant more to me than any accolades I'd previously received. In April of 2010, I was inducted into the Hall of Fame with Hugh Durham, our former basketball coach and multiple final-four coach, and the incredible Harry Sargent, CEO of a major shipping company. In attendance were the Himots, my uncle Joe, my brother, and my children, as well as my dearest friend Larry (Ace) Diamond. I took advantage of the opportunity to honor some of the FSU faculty who had done so much to encourage me. I was so proud. I only wished my parents could have been there to participate in and enjoy the event.

2010 FSU Hall of Famers

Bob & Larry Diamond

Chris, Bob & Joe Houck

2010 FSU Hall of Fame Induction

MILESTONES

In December of 2009, I was elected to the board of the Community Services Association (CSA), the property owners' association that ran Sea Pines Plantation. My three-year term would commence on January 1, 2010. Sea Pines was facing multiple challenges, including a serious lawsuit, dredging of the waterways, a massive expansion plan of the Sea Pines Resort facilities, an aging infrastructure, no long-term strategic plan, and a group of very disgruntled homeowners. By the end of my first year, I was nominated to chair the board. Along with my friend Rob Marsac, we would overcome fourteen problems in our three-year stint. I did not run for reelection as this was the most thankless undertaking I had ever pursued.

My mornings were generally pretty routine. I'd start with coffee and a crossword puzzle at Starbucks with a few friends. Starbucks was like a revolving door of Hilton Head locals, so I met a lot of people there. After coffee, I would head over to Breakthrough Fitness to work out, followed by walking the dogs, pushing some paper, and playing golf.

The morning of February 25, 2011, while I was having coffee at Starbucks, I got a call from Chris informing me that Sabelle was in the hospital and about to deliver seven weeks early. I raced home, grabbed some clothes, and was on the road in twenty minutes. Chiara was born at 9:41 a.m. in Paterson, New Jersey, and was a mere four pounds, ten ounces. She was immediately taken to the ICU. When I arrived that night, I was allowed to go in and see her in the ICU. The experience was heart wrenching. There were thirty-two babies in the ICU. Chiara's eyes were covered, and there were life support tubes coming from everywhere.

The next several days were very scary. A couple of the babies didn't make it. After several days, the hospital made Sabelle leave, which was devastating for her. Chiara was kept in the ICU for about three weeks, and Sabelle would arrive first thing in the morning and stay until late in the evening. Everyone was ecstatic when she came home.

Year 2011 also brought Elizabeth's graduation from the University of South Carolina, where her cousin Kristen had also graduated. She earned her degree in psychology with a minor in criminal justice and did it in four years. Elizabeth certainly enjoyed her college years, becoming a true Gamecock. David and Kristen, the Himots, Chris, Sabelle, Lauren, and I all attended her graduation. The speaker was George Pataki, the former governor of New York during the 9/11 attacks.

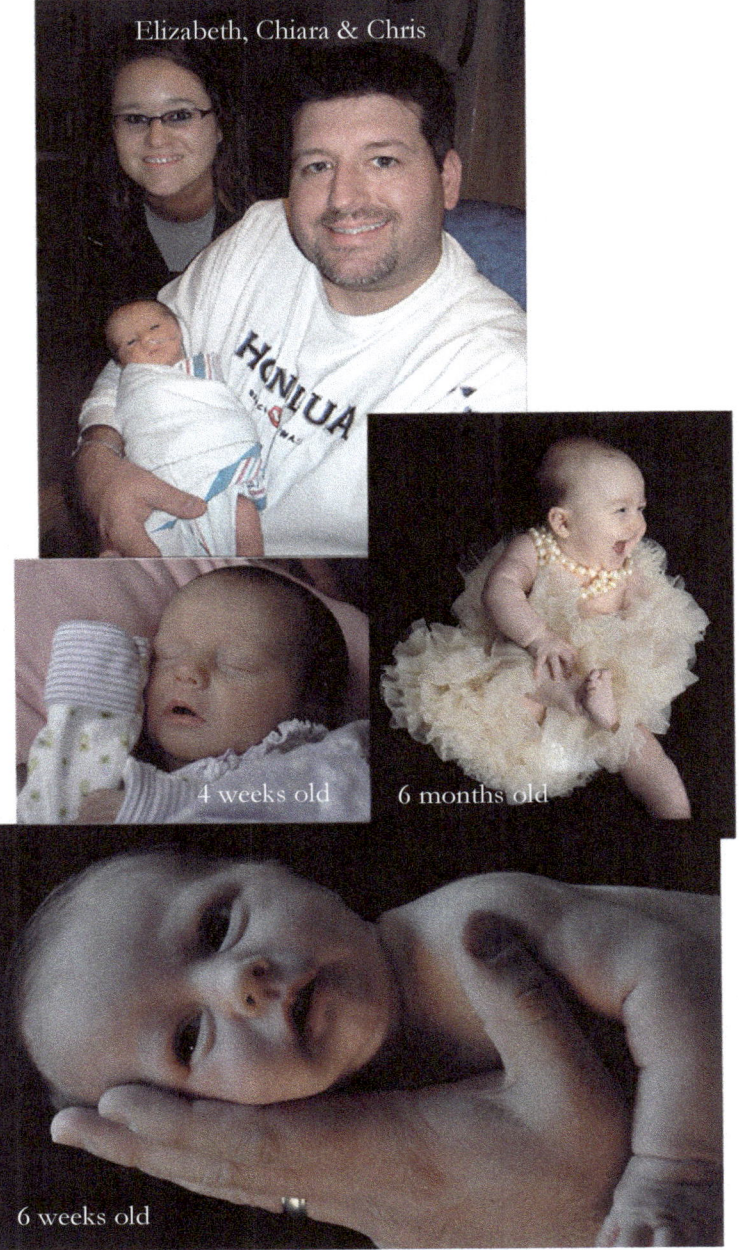

Elizabeth, Chiara & Chris

4 weeks old

6 months old

6 weeks old

The University
of
South Carolina

FIGHTING
GAMECOCK

Elizabeth's Graduation
From USC

Bob, Ann & Chiara : Disney Cruise

Bob & Chiara in Morristown

SPCC

Maui 2009

ANN

For a number of years going to Starbucks, I'd see many of the same faces coming and going. Invariably, either someone would introduce me or I'd just smile and say "good morning." I'd see some of the same faces at the gym. Ann was one of those people. I had asked about her and was told she was engaged to a polo player who worked at Lawton Stables. I knew she was quite a bit younger than me, but I just seemed intrigued by her. At some point, I heard that her fiancé had passed away of pancreatic cancer. He was only forty-three years old. While I'd continue to see her at Starbucks or the gym, I never seemed able to muster up the courage to ask her out.

One day at the gym, I was on an elliptical next to her and started up a conversation, mainly complaining about the equipment at the gym. I said I was going to quit, and she asked me where I would join. I told her I'd let her know if I found something, so she gave me her phone number. Stupid me didn't get the hint. A few months later, she asked me why I hadn't called. After bumbling my response for a minute, I told her I had put a gym in the house and asked if she'd like to see it. She said, "When?"

And I said, "How about tonight?"

We had several dates, but then I went to Mallorca and didn't see her for a while. When I returned in August, we began seeing each other very regularly, and our romance blossomed rapidly.

I asked her if she'd like to go to Paris with me, and she didn't hesitate for a minute, so we planned a great trip for November. We had a wonderful time seeing all the sights, spending days at the museums, lunching at Jules Verne at the Eiffel Tower, and cruising the Seine. We also had dinner with Ann's friends Gert and Alice, who lived just outside Paris in Meudon and would suggest we do a house swap in August.

By December, we were planning our future together. Additionally, I was busier than ever, having been elected to be a trustee of the FSU Foundation, in addition to my College of Business directorship and CSA board chairmanship.

In 2012, 2013, and 2014, we did trade houses with Gert and Alice and made several spectacular trips to France, Mallorca, Italy, and Scandinavia. We toured Versailles, the Loire Valley, the French Riviera, Normandy, Florence, Rome, Berlin, Stockholm, Helsinki, Copenhagen, Saint Petersburg, and London.

On the home front, I had had my fill of the politics of Sea Pines, so I did not run for reelection, choosing to concentrate on my work as a trustee of the FSU Foundation. I wrote the long-term strategic plan for the foundation and was later elected treasurer. And I recently completed my term as chairman of the Board of Governors of the FSU College of Business. My objectives for the college were straightforward: (1) build and fund a new College of Business building that would attract top faculty, (2) develop a program to retain and reward the best faculty, and (3) create a student learning experience that would be inclusive and interactive using the most up-to-date technology to enhance the student experience through new learning models and the expansion of honors programs.

One fabulous treat Ann and I enjoyed in January 2014 was attending the Rose Bowl in Pasadena, where FSU would play Auburn for the national championship. Auburn dominated the game, but we pulled off a spectacular fourth quarter to win the game. Jeff Rohr and his son, James, were sitting with Ann and me right on the fifty-yard line. We went berserk when we won (our third national championship).

In 2014, Ann and I began to discuss to possibility of moving to Florida. We did quite a bit of exploring on both coasts. One of the benefits of this move would be to have her girls in a much better educational environment. Being exceptional students, among other things, would allow them to apply for Bright Futures scholarships offered in the public university system in Florida.

Madison, Bob &
Lauren's Graduation

Hayes Girls

Lauren Hayes

Madison Hayes

Lauren in NYC

Bob & Ann at the Grand Canyon

Ann in France

Bob & Ann in France

Ann with the Royal Guard

Ann at the Grand Canyon

Ann in the Straw Market in Florence

Ann & Bob in New York

Anne & Bob in Tivoli

Ann & Bob
GRAND LUAU at HONUA'ULA 2013

Ann & Bob, Jockey Hollow

THE WATER CLUB, NORTH PALM BEACH

After multiple trips to southeast Florida, we found the Water Club, a high-rise complex under construction overlooking Lake Worth and Lost Tree Village. We knew the views would be spectacular, overlooking Singer Island and the Atlantic Ocean, and the builder was projecting delivery in June of 2016, giving me what I thought would be ample time to market the Hilton Head house. This would be the eighteenth time in my life I would move.

As we came back and forth to check on the progress, my great friend Bob Wechsler would put us up in his house in Lake Worth. There was a lot to consider. We would be moving from a 6,000-square-foot house into a 2,400-square-foot condo. Also, at what point would we transition the girls from Hilton Head High School to a high school here? Construction delays and Hurricane Matthew, the first hurricane to make landfall on Hilton Head Island in 124 years, threw the housing market into a tailspin, further complicating things.

We didn't close at the Water Club until January 2017 and only after multiple preclosing walk-throughs. Elizabeth and her significant other, Jason Sereno, moved to Arizona in July of 2017, where she works as a psychologist with autistic children.

Life for the past couple of years seemed to be a series of triangular trips between North Palm Beach, Hilton Head Island, and FSU in Tallahassee. I really look forward to the time when the Hilton Head property has sold. Now that Ann's girls, Madison and Lauren, are both in college we can travel more freely. In the meantime, we have managed a few great trips—two Disney cruises, a family trip to Phoenix, where Elizabeth now resides—and this past Christmas, we were all together with Chris and his family in New Jersey.

The girls both attended Dwyer High School in Florida and were accepted in the International Baccalaureate Program. Madison is attending FSU on Bright Futures and has continued to perform well academically. Lauren has chosen the University of Colorado (Boulder) because of their high rankings in aerospace engineering. Both earned their International Baccalaureate degrees. Ann and I are so proud of their achievements

THE GAME OF GOLF

I was first introduced to the wonderful game of golf when my father and godfather let me come with them to Valley Forge Golf Club. My father had a set of Sam Snead Wilson golf clubs. They let me hit a few shots on the par 3s, and I was hooked. I even bought a plastic driver and some Wiffle balls to hit in the yard.

In 1961, Jimmy Demaret, Gene Sarazen, Bob Rosburg (all famous golfers), and Jack Whitaker (a famous sports announcer) began broadcasting a TV show called *Shell's Wonderful World of Golf*. I watched it religiously. By this age, I was going to the driving range on City Avenue and playing my first full round of golf at Cobbs Creek, where I carded a cool 128. After we moved to Sarasota, as I previously mentioned, Cam gave me a set of clubs he'd had since the '30s, and his brother Larry included me in his membership at Bobby Jones Golf Course. I played every chance I got. I even got an award in high school for golf.

After college, one of my first purchases was a set of Spalding Top Flite golf clubs. I played every chance I got. Mostly, I shot in the high 80s and low 90s.

In 1972, I joined a club (Snapfinger Woods) and got my handicap to about 7 or 8 and regularly shot in the 80s. I bought new clubs at least three times. I was so obsessed that my first gift to Chris the day after his birth was a Powerbilt driver.

Over the course of my life, I had the great good fortune to play in a number of pro-ams, celebrity tournaments, and club competitions. My biggest thrill was Chris and me winning our flight at Sea Pines Country Club member-guest tournament, only to come in second in the shoot-out, losing to a long birdie putt on the eighteenth at Harbour Town. Playing with the great Jack Nicklaus in the Doral pro-am was thrilling. My parents came to follow us around, and Jack was absolutely terrific. Unfortunately, the pressure got the best of me, and I didn't play very well. Hanging around the locker room with Jack, Gary Player, Lee Trevino, J. C. Snead, Greg Norman, and Chi Chi Rodriguez was incredible.

In 1994, I was invited by the *Philadelphia Inquirer* to play in Mike Schmidt's celebrity charity event. Mike (a former Phillie) was arguably not only the greatest third baseman in the history of baseball but an exceptional golfer as well. We played together the first day, and he shot a 71. Mike introduced me to the great Yogi Berra, a lifelong hero of mine whose locker was next to me. Yogi was magnetic. He signed some baseballs for me before the second round. After the first round, I asked him how he'd played. He replied, "Kid, it's so hot out there you could sweat" (a little known Yogi-ism).

The next day, I played with Hall of Fame basketball player Charles Barkley. When I commented that he had as big a following as Jack Nicklaus, he retorted, "Well, I'm a better basketball player than he is." At the nineteenth hole, we had some fun with Tug McGraw, the great relief pitcher for the Mets and the Phillies. It was amazing.

Golf has been a big part of my life for sixty years. The one thing I miss the most, though, is playing with the marvelous Larry (Ace) Diamond, who had a hole in one at Sea Pines no. 4 when he was eighty-three. I guess there is still hope for me.

Bob, Dean Smith & Pete Dye

Sam Snead & Bob

Ann & Ricki Fowler

Pete Dye & Bob

Bob & Craig Stadler

Jack Nicklaus & Bob

Bob & Peter Jacobson

Bob, Charles Barkley & David Coradini

Bob at 18th Hole Saint Andrews Old Course

Michael Bechert, Bob & Chris

Bob at 16th Hole Cypress Point

Harbourtown Pro-Am Trophy Presentation

Doral 1990 with Peter Jacobson

John Lamb, Rod Laver, Tom Bowles & Bob
7th Tee Pebble Beach

2017 Heritage with Ernie Els

Annual Golf Outing with Zim, Lechtner & Wex
"Gopher Broke Boys"

"Gopher Broke Boys"

Bob & Chris at 18th Hole Harbourtown

Bob & The Wanamaker Trophy

MUSIC AND DANCE

My parents, as well as my father's mother, Nellie, always reinforced my love of music and dance. My father loved music and actually played the piano (although rarely). We always seemed to have music playing in the house—besides Frank Sinatra, lots of big bands.

Ferde Grofé's *Grand Canyon Suite* and Ravel's *Boléro* are what I recall listening to most often. Nellie loved musicals and encouraged me to sing. Her favorite song was "The Surrey with the Fringe on Top" from the musical *Oklahoma!* She encouraged me to sing like Elvis. Even in her seventies, she was quite the Elvis fan.

Nana had been a dancer in her youth on the London stage. She and her sister Connie had been with a famous dance troupe named the Tiller Girls and had performed at the London Palladium. My mother had studied ballet. My mother really enjoyed teaching me to dance. I learned all the steps, and to this day, music and dance brings a smile to my face.

I have always loved the Broadway musicals. A list of my favorites include: *Phantom of the Opera*, *Guys and Dolls*, *Cats*, *Spamalot*, *Hair*, *A Chorus Line*, *Annie Get Your Gun*, *Pajama Game*, *La Cage aux folles*, *Grease*, *Fiddler on the Roof*, *Jersey Boys*, and *South Pacific*.

My favorite singers still are Elvis, Frank Sinatra, Dean Martin, Sammy Davis Jr., the great Bobby Short, John Gary, Bob Dylan, Johnny Mathis, and Bobby Rydell. My favorite bands would be the Beatles and the Rolling Stones.

Best Dance Partner Ever:
Sue Nodine

Elizabeth & Bob

Chris & Lauren

Elizabeth & Larry Diamond

Lauren & Bob

Still Dancing

FSU, 2006–NOW

My return to Florida State has been most gratifying. Involvement on the Board of Governors of the College of Business, selection to the Hall of Fame, and becoming a trustee of the foundation continues to be extremely rewarding. It has been a great joy to be invited as a guest lecturer and engage with today's students. Before opening the floor to questions, I leave the students with these thoughts:

My Eight Habits for Professional Success

1. Demonstrate initiative and leadership.
2. Distinguish yourself among your peers.
3. Focus on delivering a superior performance.
4. Surround yourself with competent people.
5. Work collaboratively.
6. Inspire others to share your vision.
7. Think like your boss.
8. Inspect what you expect.

SOME PERSONAL ADVICE

1. Do what you love and love what you do; you'll be a lot happier.
2. Reach for the stars; you might just catch one.
3. Don't take others for granted.
4. Treat others as you'd like to be treated.
5. Never assume anything.
6. Out of adversity comes resolve, and out of resolve comes success.

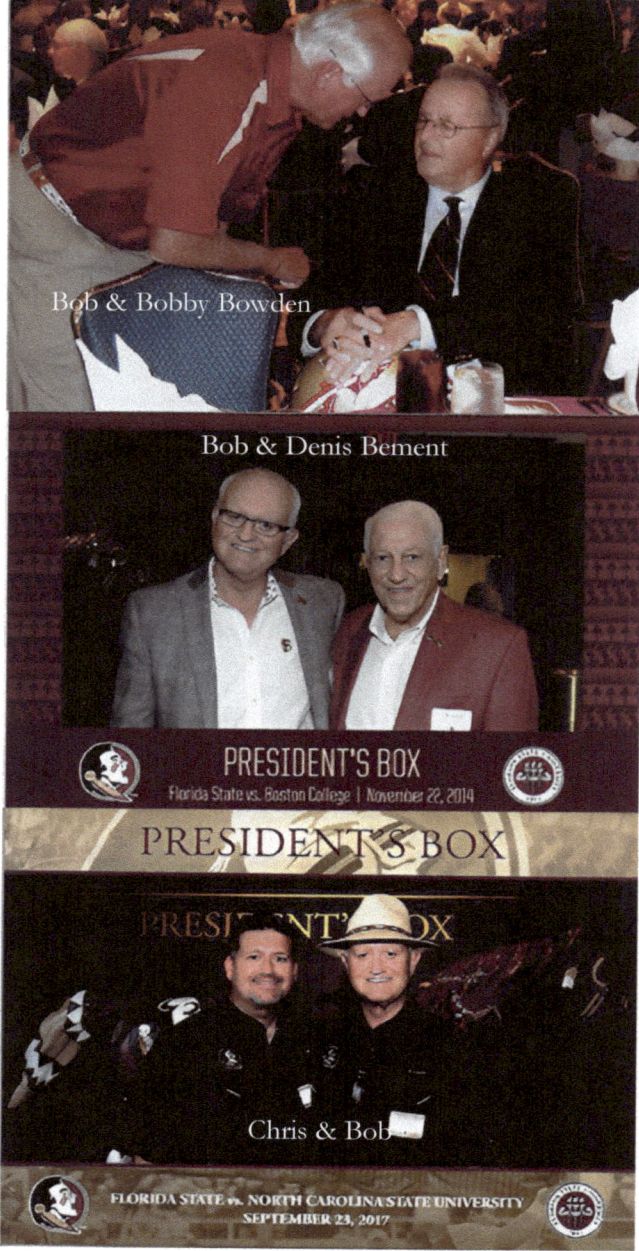

Bob & Bobby Bowden

Bob & Denis Bement

PRESIDENT'S BOX
Florida State vs. Boston College | November 22, 2014

PRESIDENT'S BOX

Chris & Bob

FLORIDA STATE vs. NORTH CAROLINA STATE UNIVERSITY
SEPTEMBER 23, 2017

FSU national Championship Game 2013 Season

Jeff & James Rohr

Chief Osceola &
Renegade

THE VIEW FROM FORTY THOUSAND FEET

Here are a few comments on what I attribute my career success to:

- Effective management depends on solid decision-making.
- Solid decision-making is the result of the analysis of valid data and evaluation of other available pertinent information.
- Probe deeply, question skeptically, and bring things to a conclusion.
- Avoid analysis paralysis.
- Be sure that each decision fits into your long-term objectives to achieve success.
- Keep your eye on the goal.
- Observing the way people behave is much more important than what they have to say. True character revolves around understanding the needs of others and engaging them without compromising your own standards. As Richard Mandel (headmaster at Friends Select, where

Chris attended sixth and seventh grade) once told me, the key to success is to challenge and support. It's easy to challenge people. The key is to support them in their endeavors.

- Embrace the rules and behave ethically. Your reputation is at stake, and its value is immeasurable.

Businesses are a compilation of assets, mostly inert ones like physical plant, systems, equipment, and inventory. The single most important asset is people, the asset of human resources, the energy people provide that creates and directs inertia. People energize every business plan. The most valuable tool in leadership is understanding how to inspire people and support their unique contributions.

In support of the contributions of the people who dedicated their livelihoods to Woodies and Wanamaker's before and during the Chapter 11 process of selling the companies, we were able to retain ten thousand jobs, certainly one of the most significant accomplishments of my career.

LOVE AND LIFE

I've had the great experience to have observed so many positive technological advances in my life, and I'm continually amazed—passenger jets, color TV, computers (once the size of a room that now fit into your hand), the digital age, rockets landing people on the moon, and space stations. Investing in innovation yields some extraordinary results. Many of the comforts of life we enjoy today were merely ideas in 1945. I believe the single greatest advancement in my life has been in the medical research and health field, without a doubt the unraveling of the genetic code being the most significant. It will change the longevity and quality of life for centuries to come.

It seems to me that one of the great joys in life is to experience unconditional love. Parents almost always love their children without condition. Dogs teach us unconditional love too. Somewhere along this winding road of life, you may be blessed with the joy of true love from a spouse, a child, or even a friend. It's so worth embracing, for it is truly rare.

Love is the most complex emotion, very difficult to describe; sometimes it wounds us, but it's worth the risk. Love is the only tie that truly binds our souls. Love with all your being and live a life that positively affects everyone you touch.

ETERNITY

When I was about twelve, I asked my uncle Jack what I thought to be a most profound question. "Where is heaven?" After a little further probing, I wanted to know where the universe ended. He responded by explaining to me that "there are just some things that our minds can't comprehend." That statement led me to a lifelong interest in observing my environment and trying to validate the concept of blind faith, the foundation of all religious belief.

Here's what I have concluded: The synergies in life are truly a wonder—male/ female and plant/animal, for example. There are other opposites to contemplate too—good/evil, love/hate. I continue to be overwhelmed by the broad spectrum of talent that exists. The human race couldn't exist without it. My uncle Jack was right; there are concepts that are too vast for our minds to comprehend. For me, though, it's enough to know that this amazing existence we live couldn't be an accident. Just to know that one of the great joys of life is procreation validates my blind faith.

The great gifts I've had in my life begin with the gift of life from my parents and the gift I've had of parenting happy, healthy children. All the wonders of a fulfilling life start with love and family.

EPILOGUE

Although my story is largely based on my great, good fortune in life and how it has affected my career and lifestyle, by far, the greatest joy and most fulfilling part of my life has been the unbelievable gift of parenting three amazing children, all of whom I'm incredibly proud.

My firstborn, Chris, has set such a beautiful stage for me to learn how to become a great father. The pure pleasure of guiding his growth and observing his development as a young man, adult, husband, and father has been rewarding and gratifying beyond description. As a child, he was happy, active, enthusiastic, and participative, whether in sports, biking, boating, fishing, or Indian Guides. Chris is a model husband, father, son, and friend with impeccable values. He has "all the right stuff."

My daughter Lauren has been a true delight. Her inquisitive nature, her high level of energy, her participative style, her creativity, and her level of intelligence have been a joy to observe. Lauren responds to every challenge with courage, love, and conviction. Over the years, she has developed a cadre of very loyal friends. I believe it's because she is such a great friend to have. The quality of her character is reflected in everything she pursues. I'm so proud of the truly lovely woman she's become.

Elizabeth, my miracle child, is a true wonder. She has very deep, altruistic feelings. Her mother's long-term illness was overwhelming for her to cope with, yet she has remained optimistic. She kept her mother so busy being a mommy that we all seemed to live a reasonably normal life. Elizabeth has been committed to helping disadvantaged children since her college graduation, and she is beginning to work her own miracles.

All three of my offspring embody the best tenets of great character. They love one another and everyone in the family without condition. They encourage one another and love to participate in family time together. I'm proud of their honesty, integrity, generosity, and respectful nature and inspired by their love of dogs.

I once heard that when you have children, your love doesn't add; it multiplies. With the subsequent birth of each of my children, I have found that to be true; but with the birth of my granddaughter, I have found that my love for my family has grown exponentially. I have never quite felt old enough to be a grandparent or understood what it really meant to be one. Nevertheless, at age sixty-five, it happened.

As a youngster, my grandmother (Nellie) had regularly told me I was the joy of her life. I don't think I understood that until I became a grandfather. Participating in Chiara's life has added joy and purpose to my life. From the day of her birth, I've reveled in her growth. Of course, she's the most beautiful little girl in the world (no bias there). In addition, I marvel at her inquisitive nature, her naturally loving temperament, and her intelligence. Her energy level on a scale of 1 to 10 is at least a 12. She is an exceptionally vibrant young lady. My hope and dream for her is that she will continue to exhibit the marvelous qualities that she has demonstrated in the first eight and a half years of her life. What a true joy it will be for me if I can continue to participate actively in her development for many years to come. Being Chiara's daddy's daddy (DD) is truly fulfilling. I love every minute of it.

Pinch me! I must be dreaming.

Christopher Patrick Mang

Christopher Patrick Mang

Lauren Elise Mang

Lauren Elise Mang

Sarah Elizabeth Mang

Sarah Elizabeth Mang

Sea Pines

Age 2

Age 3

Age 4

Age 5

Age 6

Age 7

Elizabeth & Lucy

Brando

Brando & Abby

Family Thanksgiving Sedoma, AZ

Family Christmas 2018 in NYC,
At Ground Zero